Fresh Ideas for Designing With Black, White and Gray

Fresh Ideas For Designing With Black, White and Gray

GAIL DEIBLER FINKE

NORTH LIGHT BOOKS
CINCINNATI, OHIO

This hardcover edition of *Fresh Ideas for Designing With Black, White and Gray* features a "self-jacket" that eliminates the need for a separate dust jacket. It provides sturdy protection for your book while it saves paper, trees and energy.

Other fine North Light Books are available from your local bookstore, art supply store or direct from the publisher.

00   99   98   97   96   5   4   3   2   1

Library of Congress Cataloging-in-Publication Data

Finke, Gail.
     Fresh ideas for designing with black, white, and gray / Gail Deibler Finke. — 1st ed.
        p.   cm.
     Includes index.
     ISBN 0-89134-700-3 (pob : alk. paper)
     1. Graphic arts—Technique. 2. Black in art. 3. White in art. I. Title.
NC1000.F56   1996
741.6—dc20   95-37745
                                         CIP

Edited by Lynn Haller
Interior design by Sandy Conopeotis Kent
Cover design by Lamson Design

The permissions beginning on page 130 constitute an extension of this copyright page.

North Light Books are available for sales promotions, premiums and fundraising use. Special editions or book excerpts can also be created to specification. For details, contact the Special Sales Manager, F&W Publications, 1507 Dana Avenue, Cincinnati, Ohio 45207.

Acknowledgments

Thanks to all the talented designers whose work appears in this book—they truly show how much can be done with "just" black and white. Thanks also to the following people, without whom this book would have been finished far past deadline: Scott, Verna, Kelley, Amy and Karen Finke, and Phyllis Deibler.

Table of Contents

Introduction

All designers know that sometimes, particularly in low-budget projects, there are no practical alternatives to designing in black and white. It's cheap, and using screens to create one or more grays allows enough variety to satisfy the soul who craves something less stark.

But smart designers know that sometimes, even for deep-pocket clients, there are no better alternatives to designing in black and white. It can be classic, elegant and timeless—or bold, innovative and up-to-the-minute. It can communicate a variety of moods and styles, emulating the crisp efficiency of corporate communications or the amateur, hand-done look of photocopied posters for college bands.

Look around you, however, and you'll find that most designers use black and white when they have to, then abandon it for the flash and excitement of color whenever they have the chance. It takes some designers years to discover the sophisticated possibilities in black, white, and all the shades between. Once they make that discovery, however, they return to black, white and gray with renewed energy, harnessing its power for their clients.

That's why most black and white design is either poor or great. And that's why it's important to study the best of design in black, white and gray. Once you understand the medium's potential, you may find yourself turning to black, white and gray when you don't "have" to. Even if you still prefer to work in color, your black and white work will be stronger, more enjoyable to do, and better for your clients.

Designing
With
Black, White
and Gray

Using black ink and white paper actually gives a designer more options than choosing any one colored ink and any one colored paper. Colors carry inherent limits and unwritten rules: While bright yellow paper or green ink can convey many messages, both also carry emotional connotations that make them unable to convey other messages.

Black and white doesn't have those limits. It's so versatile that we accept it in almost any situation. Stark black and white provide all the palette many designers need to create powerful, memorable messages. Other designers rely on the infinite shades of gray between pure black and pure white to create complex, layered graphics with great visual depth. There's no wrong way to use black, white and gray—except, perhaps, not to use it.

Just as writing for an orchestra allows a composer to coordinate the sounds of many different instruments, so does using a variety of colors allow designers to create rich and varied works. But a composer must think differently to write a solo for one instrument. Instead of many different musical voices, he or she must highlight only one—finding the depth and variation within it. In many ways, the solo composition is a greater test of skill, because there is less to distract the listener from the structure of the composition.

Designing with black and white is much the same. The designer's challenge is to find everything he or she needs within strict limits. The underlying design must be strong, because viewers can't be distracted by a bold stroke of red or a flashy, fluorescent paper.

The same design executed in black and white or in colored inks will look very different. To bring this home, try creating a simple design in black and white, and then try it in several color combinations. Each color variation will bring with it a different mood and emotional response. But when you look at the black-and-white piece, you focus more on its composition and what it says.

Working in black and white makes other demands as well. The design tools are no different from those in any other job: type, copy, photography, illustration and space. But unless the desired look is low-budget or "not designed," black and white demands extra precision, both in production and in printing.

Creating a Mood

Although black and white do not call up emotions as strong as those awakened by colors, they are also associated with moods. An all-black page communicates mystery, elegance and (frequently) expense. An all-white page communicates purity, crispness and (frequently) no expense. But mix the two, and you can get the cut-rate look of a generic package or the intimidating and expensive feel of an annual report.

Grays can also create mood. Comforting and reliable, pure grays remind viewers

of industry and business, as well as natural objects such as ashes and stone. Match grays, though more expensive to use, carry other connotations: Brown-grays are cool and neutral, red-grays are warm and inviting. Combine black, white and gray with artful composition, and you can create a variety of moods to enhance those created by type, copy and artwork.

White Space, Black Space, Gray Space

Part of creating a mood is the amount of space surrounding the type and other design elements. Tiny type floating in an expanse of white space is a time-honored look for upscale advertisements. In a crowded magazine or newspaper, it contrasts sharply with the surrounding print and demands attention. Tiny white type on an all-black page is a popular variation, and white or black type on a gray field is a lesser-used, but equally viable, option.

Most pieces, however, need more than just a few words of type. But white, black or gray space is still important. A large amount of space gives a piece a clean, uncluttered look. It emphasizes the type or artwork, allows the underlying grid or structure to be expressed, and frequently gives a piece an air of importance. All these qualities are magnified when a piece is in black and white.

Little space left between or around design elements creates a "busy" look that can be exciting or intimidating, depending on how it's done. And little or no space left between elements creates a frenetic feel that can be overwhelming. One popular "misuse" of space is to layer type in many different sizes and shades of gray until it becomes nearly (and in some cases actually) unreadable. Viewers often react strongly to this kind of design—they will either find it irresistible or disgusting.

Type: Shape and Mass

The bewildering array of typefaces available today makes type more expressive

than ever before. Black-and-white design emphasizes the shape and weight of letters, making it the ideal medium for the type lover. Classic faces, hand-lettering and avant-garde computer fonts all do their part to make maximum impact in black and white.

Especially in all-type layouts, black-and-white designs are particularly suited to mixing faces, varying sizes and using unusual placement. Type can meander across a page or form shapes. Blocks of text can form shapes, or words can be sprinkled about artfully. The addition of boxes and lines can create a "flowchart" look, while calligraphic flourishes create the opposite impression: human and impulsive.

Photography and Illustration

Black-and-white illustration—whether pen-and-ink, block printing, scratchboard, or any number of other styles—is ideally suited for black-and-white design. Often, the artist originally creates in black and white, balancing white space and black ink as part of the process.

Though photography might seem equally suitable, it's not as well matched as you might think. Convert a black-and-white photograph to a black halftone, and you lose much of the contrast and character of fine photography. But if reproducing fine photography isn't your goal, simple halftones of black-and-white photos offer many design possibilities.

For truly fine reproduction of black-and-white photographs, many designers and printers actually turn to four-color printing. A less expensive alternative is to specify a duotone, using a second screen of gray, black or metallic inks to give the photograph depth and clarity. Similarly, a tritone uses three screens, and a quadratone uses four—both with corresponding increases in reproduction quality and, of course, cost.

Once you've mastered the challenges of black-and-white design, you might find

Envisioning a New Federal Courthouse   A PUBLIC FORUM

February 15, 1995

civic architecture

Both an illustration and a photograph are ghosted to provide visual interest to this postcard.

yourself preferring it to color. But before you create your next black-and-white masterpiece, don't forget to ask yourself the all-important question: Can it be printed?

Tips for Printing Black, White and Gray

As with any printing job, it's best to talk to your printer before you finish your design. Your printer can tell you what will—and more importantly, what won't—reproduce well using his or her equipment and the paper you specify. While offset printing is still the most common method for typical graphic design projects, remember that other methods, such as screenprinting, might be better for particular designs. And remember, too, that although black and white is often the medium of choice for inexpensive projects, achieving a special effect might make a black-and-white print job expensive.

The following is a list of printing terms and techniques that are particularly useful in black-and-white design. Because printing costs vary due to differences in

equipment, press time and geographic regions, estimates are approximate; talk with your printer about fees. And finally, to avoid disappointment, be sure to get the right kind of proof from your printer and check it carefully.

Debossing

Less popular than embossing but using a similar technique, debossing creates a "sunken" image using metal dies and heat. Costs are similar. See embossing for details.

Double Hit or Bump

A double hit or bump is a second run of the same color. It ensures that a color is bright and clear, but costs the same as a second color. A double hit is often necessary when printing blocks of white ink, or to get a rich, highly saturated block of black.

Dry Trap

Often used for varnishes, dry trapping means printing a second color over a first that has fully dried. It produces glossy

color and clean edges, but costs nearly as much as two print jobs because, to the printer, that's what it is.

Duotone

Typically used for reproducing photography, a duotone image is produced by using two halftones and two colors of ink, often gray and black or two strengths of black. It gives the photograph greater depth and clarity, but costs about twice as much as a simple black halftone.

Embossing

Many effects are possible with this technique, which produces raised type or graphics with heat and metal dies. Blind embossing, which creates a bas-relief effect, is an enduring classic. Dies begin at less than two hundred dollars, but can cost more than two thousand dollars. Choose a strong paper, leave space between the embossment and any printed matter to account for the paper's movement, and remember that an embossment looks smaller than a printed image the same size.

This postcard artfully employs black space and reversed-out type
on the front, and plenty of white space on the back.

Foil Stamping

Similar to embossing, this process stamps thin foils to the paper with a hot metal die. Unlike a blind embossment, however, a foil-stamped image looks larger after it's stamped. Metallic, clear, colored and patterned foils are available in various finishes. Die costs are similar to those used for embossing; foil cost varies with the type used.

Ghost Image

A faint, unintentional copy of an image that appears elsewhere on a piece, a ghost image is a product of the offset printing process and can be a particular hazard in black-and-white design. It's created by a large, dense image, such as a black bar or shape, which prints again as the blanket revolves. It's most visible on plain white paper.

Ghosting

A deliberate ghost effect is produced by overprinting two colors at different percentages; just be sure to print the darker ink first. Another meaning for "ghosting" is printing an image at a light screen tint, so that other images can be printed over it.

Grays: Match vs. Black

Screen tints of black are inexpensive, because you pay only for the shooting of the dot screen, and can create the effect of a second color (or colors) without the added expense. However, while innumerable grays can be created with screen tints, many of these are indistinguishable from each other; when creating a layered design, check with your printer before specifying too many such grays, to be sure that you aren't wasting money shooting screens that will end up looking the same. On the other hand, using a match gray instead of a screen of black will add the cost of a second color to your budget, but will also allow for a hint of warm or cool tone.

Halftone

A halftone uses a screen of dots to photographically reproduce continuous-tone art, such as a photograph, as a series of dots. Various sizes and patterns of screens are available; some can produce special effects. Halftones don't reproduce well on thick, porous papers.

Opacity

A measure of how opaque a paper or ink is. Paper opacity must always be considered when speccing a job, since show-through of a design from one side of a page to another may be desirable (when planned) or undesirable (when not, or when it interferes with the look or legibility of the material printed on the other side). Ink opacity is equally important, especially when printing large blocks of ink, or printing lighter colored inks on darker colored paper—in the first case, a less opaque ink might produce a blotchy block of color, and in the second case, the paper might show through and dull the ink's color. In both cases, a more opaque ink, or a double hit of a less opaque ink, may be necessary to achieve the look you want; check with your printer.

Reverse

Reversed-out type is produced by printing the area around the type, allowing another color or the paper to show through; reverses are one of the most common ways to add contrast and variety to a black-and-white design with few graphics. However, because ink spreads or "bleeds," thin lines can be lost; good typefaces for this treatment are those with fairly thick lines and curves.

Screen Tint

Like a halftone, screen tints create lighter swatches of a given color by printing dots instead of solid ink. The density of the dots determines the strength of the color.

Varnishes

Protective and decorative varnishes come in many finishes, from high gloss to matte, and can be tinted with colored or metallic inks. Varnishes are often used to add contrast and crispness to a piece. There are two processes: Spot varnish, often used over artwork, costs about as much as a second color; full-coat varnish, which covers a whole page, is less expensive because it is simpler to do.

White

The most common way to use white on a printed piece is to leave some areas of white paper unprinted. You can print white ink on gray or black, but because white ink is frequently less opaque than colored ink, you may need to print the white twice, which would cost as much as two extra colors.

Posters

While most people think of posters as an opportunity for splashy color and garish graphics, black-and-white posters can make just as much of a graphic impact when done well. The mood of a black-and-white poster is different—cooler, starker and more mysterious. But despite—or perhaps because of—their rarity, black-and-white posters can command attention, especially when surrounded by the four-color posters that are their usual competition for a viewer's attention.

Many of the posters shown here depend on one simple image and a great deal of white space to achieve impact. Because of its size, a poster can use this design effect to its best advantage—a large trim size allows more than enough room for plenty of information, and lots of white space to emphasize it.

First Presbyterian Church

Art Director/Studio Stephen Brower/Stephen Brower Design
Designer/Studio Stephen Brower/Stephen Brower Design
Illustrator Stephen Brower
Client/Service First Presbyterian Church/church
Paper Cougar
Type Caslon 540
Ink Black on white
Printing Offset
Software None

Concept For this poster advertising a concert of religious songs, the designer relied on white space and a strong illustration to deliver big impact on a small budget. The imaginative illustration fuses two images, a musical staff and a crucifix, with simplicity and elegance.
Cost $165
Print Run 400

A
CELEBRATION
OF
SONG
IN
HIS
NAME

SATURDAY † FEBRUARY 13TH † 7:30 PM † FIRST PRESBYTERIAN CHURCH
ROUTE 34 & FRANKLIN STREET † MATAWAN

Design by Steven Brower

Theater Schmeater

Art Directors/Studio Randy Lim, Jesse Doquilo, Glenn Mitsui/Studio MD
Designer/Studio Randy Lim/Studio MD
Illustrator Randy Lim
Client/Service Theater Schmeater/theater company
Type Matrix Wide
Ink Black on white
Printing Blackline Diazo
Software Aldus FreeHand, Adobe Photoshop

Concept An unusual and inexpensive printing method gives this theater poster its distinction. In its layered imagery, the design suggests the opening credits of the play's namesake television show, which was also produced in black and white.
Special Printing Technique The deep, saturated black ink produced by using the diazo process (similar to blueprint production) gives the design its impact. As velvety as screenprinting ink, the black ink makes the reversed-out title shine as if it were overprinted.
Print Run 500

Tracy Wong Lecture

Art Director/Studio Bob Barrie/
Fallon McElligott
Designer/Studio Bob Barrie/Fallon
McElligott
Copywriter Doug de Grood
Client/Service Art Director's/
Copywriter's Club/professional
organization
Ink Black on off-white
Printing Offset

Concept This poster/invitation for a
speech by designer Tracy Wong par-
odies his style while imitating it well.
Like many all-type designs, this one
benefits from black-and-white pre-
sentation because the reader can
view the type without being distracted by color.
Cost Design, printing and typeset-
ting donated
Print Run 1,000

Yikes! Have
you noticed that
a lot of ads lately start
out with really big type which
gets progressively smaller as you
work your way down the page? Good agencies
are doing it. Mediocre agencies are doing it. Even
really lame agencies are doing it. Why? Some might call it a trend.

Others, a breakthrough. Whatever. Love it. Hate it. The truth is, it can and

has been done well. Most notably by the creator of the Nature Company ads, Tracy Wong, who (all these

types of ads come to a point eventually) will be speaking to the Art Directors/Copywriters Club, Thursday, November 14.

Tracy, for those of you who think "CA" stands for "California," is an art director at Goodby, Berlin & Silverstein in San Francisco. Oh, and he's not a girl, as his name might

suggest. Although he does have a ponytail. This type is getting really squinty now, so we'll wrap it up: Azur Restaurant. 5:30 Cocktails. 6, dinner. 7, Tracy. 20 bucks for non-members. Members free. RSVP by Nov. 12, 339-1590. Futura Extra-Bold Condensed lives!

Tracy Wong at the Art Directors/Copywriters Club, Nov. 14.

Type: P&H/Letterwox   Printing: Franklin Press   Concept: Bob & Doug

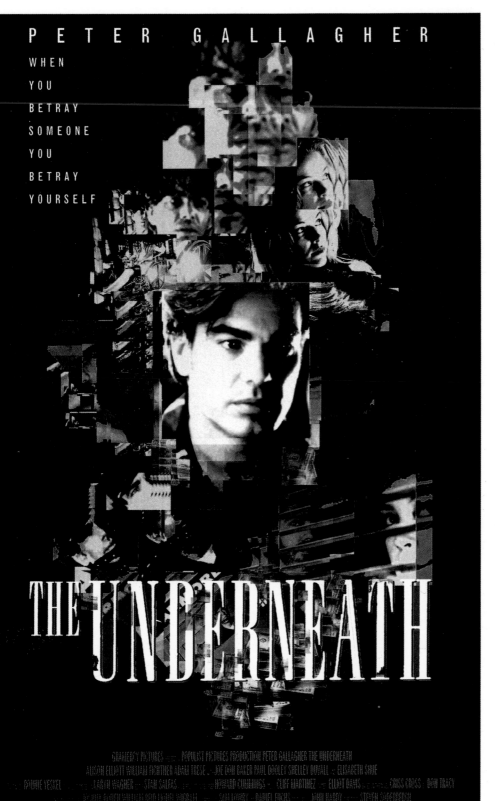

The Underneath

Art Director/Studio Mike Salisbury/Mike Salisbury Communications Inc.
Designer/Studio Mary Evelyn McGough/Mike Salisbury Communications Inc.
Photographer Alan Pappé
Client/Product Gramercy/motion pictures
Type Grotesque Condensed
Ink Black and spot varnish on white
Printing Offset
Software Adobe Photoshop, QuarkXPress

Concept For this movie poster, bluish black tones and layered images create an arty, film noir look. The stars' faces, depicted in provocative settings or with concerned expressions, suggest that the film concerns psychological, as well as physical, danger. The short copy hints at the plot without revealing the story. This image was also adapted for newspaper and magazine ads, a compact disc cover, a book cover, a video box, and sales and advertising displays.
Cost $250,000

Bernard Maisner Studio

Art Director/Studio Bernard
Maisner/Bernard Maisner Studio
Designer/Studio Helane Blumfield/
Helane Blumfield Photography
Photographer Helane Blumfield
Client/Service Bernard Maisner
Studio/handlettering; Helane
Blumfield Photography/photography
Type Garamond
Software QuarkXPress
Printing Rappaport Stonetone
Process

Concept This image, which ran as a
full-page ad in a design magazine and
was sent to potential clients as a
poster, highlighted the work of both
creators. The theme "body and soul,"
expressed by both the model's pensive pose and the hand-lettered quotations that twine around her body,
elevates the image to a spiritual plane.
Design Strategy Black and white
abstracts the figure and helps rein-
force the poster's serious, respectful
tone. The photograph's graininess
adds to the mood.
Cost $10,000
Print Run 4,000

Sommese Design

Art Directors/Studio Lanny
Sommese, Kristin Sommese/
Sommese Design
Designer/Studio Kristin
Sommese/Sommese Design
Illustrator Lanny Sommese
Client/Service Sommese
Design/graphic design
Paper French Speckletone
Type Avant Garde Regular and Demi
Ink Black on white
Printing Screenprinting
Software Aldus PageMaker

Concept White space and humorous,
single-line drawings are key to the
success of this series of three posters,
sent to current and prospective
clients. The illustrations play off the
description "a wife and husband
design partnership," a reversal of the
standard description. In each case, the
illustrations' punchlines are found in
the positive and negative spaces
where the figures merge.

Design Strategy Rather than depending on dense images and type, this
series hangs delicate type and illustration in a sea of white space, relying
on fine balance and contrast. Copy
and a logo in the upper left is balanced
by the firm's name, hand-lettered, in
the bottom right. Both are secondary
to the central images, which are
composed of narrow broken lines.
Cost $500

Planned Parenthood of Iowa

Art Director/Studio John Sayles/ Sayles Graphic Design

Designer/Studio John Sayles/Sayles Graphic Design

Illustrator John Sayles

Client/Service Planned Parenthood of Greater Iowa/family planning

Paper James River Curtis Linen

Type Hand-rendered

Ink Match silver-gray on black

Printing Screenprinted

Software None

Concept Part of an extensive campaign celebrating Planned Parenthood of Iowa's 60th anniversary, this series of posters had to be economical for mass distribution. All three 13½ x 20 posters were printed on one sheet. The designer suggested creating three different designs and printing 500 of each, rather than printing 1,500 of the same design, for more variety. The rest of the campaign— which included a limited-edition poster, an invitation, a program and custom pins—was color, with black, avocado, copper and silver as the primary palette.

Design Strategy Using black paper sidesteps problems typically encountered when trying to create a consistent black, and the density of the gray screenprinting ink keeps the copy and illustration crisp and stylish.

Print Run 500 each

THE BREATHTAKING VIEWS.

THE ROMANTIC SUNSETS.

THE SPIT DROPPING FROM 2,000 FEET.

Join us for a memorable flight over the Saint Croix Valley, where the sky WIEDERKEHR BALLOON RIDES *really is the limit to your enjoyment. For flight information, just call 436-8172.*

Weiderkehr Balloon Rides

Art Director/Studio Joe Paprocki/ Fallon McElligott

Copywriter Doug de Grood

Illustrator Bob Blewett

Client/Service Weiderkehr Balloon Rides/hot air balloon rides

Type Madrome

Ink Black on off-white

Printing Offset

Software None

Concept The look of nineteenth-century engravings is a natural one for black-and-white design, as this poster for a hot air balloon enterprise shows. The old-fashioned type, illustration and faux woodcut marks match the design with the subject, which itself has a nineteenth-century feel.

Communities Caring for Children

Art Director/Studio Dean Hanson/ Fallon McElligott

Copywriter Doug de Grood

Photographers Ripsaw Photography/ Shawn Michenzi (coffin); Halsey Creative Services (clipboard)

Client/Service Communities Caring for Children/advocacy group

Type Bodega

Ink Black, match gray and varnish on white

Printing Offset

Concept Photography is paramount on these posters, which promote regular doctor visits and immunizations for infants. Duotones make the photographs deeper and richer, while varnish helps them stand out.

Design Strategy Both life-sized posters depend on shock value for their effectiveness. Therefore, crisp photography and outstanding reproduction are vital to their success.

Print Run 1,000 each

(Actual Size)

Childhood diseases like whooping cough and measles can be life threatening. They're also 100% preventable. Give your baby a shot at life; have him immunized. For assistance, call the number below. [place sticker here]

When's The Last Time Your Baby Had A Checkup?

Your baby may be small, but her health needs are great. For help finding a doctor or for more information call the number below. [place sticker here]

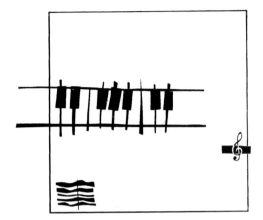

Atlanta Symphony Orchestra

Art Director/Studio Jan Lorenc/ Lorenc Design

Designers/Studio Jan Lorenc, Florence Wetterwald/Lorenc Design

Client/Service Atlanta Symphony Orchestra/orchestra

Paper Champion Kromekote

Type Helvetica Ultra Bold Condensed

Ink Black on white

Printing Offset

Software QuarkXPress

Concept Winners of a monthly black-and-white poster design contest for the Atlanta Symphony Orchestra, these two pieces use black and white to symbolize music. One poster uses white space in an imaginative illustration based on piano keys, while the other plays with musical scores, which are traditionally printed in black on white.

Special Production Techniques The piano key illustration was done on hand-cut paper, and blown up on a photocopier to emphasize the imperfections.

Print Run 1,000

French Paper

Art Director/Studio Charles
Anderson/Charles S. Anderson
Design Co.
Designers/Studio Charles Anderson,
Joel Templin/Charles S. Anderson
Design Co.
Client/Product French Paper Co./
paper
Paper French Newsprint White
Type Prestige Elite, TW Century,
Memphis
Ink Black on white
Printing Screenprinting
Software Aldus FreeHand

Concept Originally run as a full-page
advertisement in *Emigré* magazine,
this image was so popular that it was
repeated as an oversized, limited-
edition poster. At 51½" x 34¾", the
size of the poster gives the raw,
Modernist-inspired imagery even
more power, as does the dense black
ink created by screenprinting.

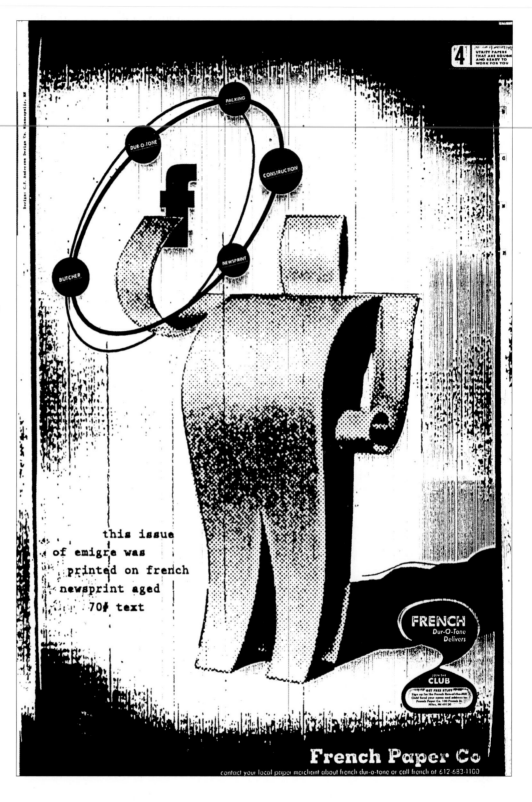

SHAKESPEARE SERIES, PAVILION THEATRE, JUNE 11 & 12, 8 PM.

MACBETH

SHAKESPEARE SERIES, PAVILION THEATRE, JUNE 4 & 5, 8 PM.

ROMEO AND JULIET

Pennsylvania State University Theatre Department

Art Director/Studio Lanny Sommese/ Sommese Design

Designer/Studio Lanny Sommese/ Sommese Design

Illustrator Lanny Sommese

Client/Service Pennsylvania State University Theatre Department/ theater education

Paper French Speckletone

Type Handcut paper and antique typewriter

Ink Black on white

Printing Screenprinting

Software None

Concept In both theater posters, type and illustration play with positive and negative space. The illustration for *Romeo and Juliet* distills the love and death intertwined in Shakespeare's play to one simple image. The illustration for *Macbeth*, presented in an unusual horizontal format, contains a "hidden" picture. At first glance, viewers might see only the dead king's face. A second look reveals his killer's face silhouetted against his crown, showing in one image the play's theme of betrayal and regicide.

Special Production Technique The illustrations were created with cut and torn paper, giving them a naive look that belies their sophisticated messages. Their mass makes them suited to black-and-white reproduction, and the screenprinting process helps ensure even expanses of dense black ink.

Cost $150 (each)

Print Run 100

Showcase:
Black and White
in Color

Ironically, sometimes the best way to show black-and-white design is through color photographs. To be appreciated, a black-and-white design element has to be seen with the color it contrasts with, and a black-and-white sign needs to be seen against the color surrounding it. A match gray has to be matched, and a duotone, tri-tone or four-color reproduction of a black-and-white photo has to be reproduced as faithfully as possible.

This section shows black-and-white design at work in many ways. The publications, products, and even UPC bar codes showcased here prove that, from packaging to signage, black and white is always appropriate. Like the little black dress, you can dress it up or down for any occasion.

Art Direction

Art Director/Studio Andrea Fridley/
Art Direction magazine
Designer/Studio Andrea Fridley/*Art Direction* magazine
Photographer Lawrence Scaduto
Client/Service *Art Direction* magazine/trade publication
Type Gill Sans Bold
Ink Four-color process
Printing Offset
Software QuarkXPress

Concept The photograph on this magazine cover was not commissioned, but was chosen from the photographer's portfolio. The art director chose a black-and-white photo to represent the season: the end of winter leading to the hope of spring. The shadowy figure can also be read as a sly reference to Punxatawny Phil and Groundhog Day.

Special Production Technique The art director chose to reproduce the black-and-white original by four-color process. This adds a warm tone to the photo, and effectively captures the picture's eye-fooling, three-dimensional effect.

Print Run 8,000

FEBRUARY 1995 · THE MAGAZINE OF VISUAL COMMUNICATION · $4.50

Safari Golf Company

Art Directors/Studio Mamoru
Shimokochi, Ann Reeves/
Shimokochi/Reeves
Designer/Studio Mamoru
Shimokochi/Shimokochi/Reeves
Client/Service The Safari Golf
Company/golf apparel manufacturer
Type Garamond Condensed
Software Adobe Illustrator

Concept The designer chose black
and white to give maximum strength
to his design, which was used as a
signature for the client's line of golf
apparel. The memorable identity features a gorilla's head with a spiky
"halo," a humorous but bold image.

YMCA of Greater Toronto

Art Directors/Studio Diti Katona, John Pylypczak/Concrete Design Communications Inc.
Designers/Studio Renata Chubb, John Pylypczak/Concrete Design Communications Inc.
Photographers John Pylypczak, Diti Katona, Roman Pylypczak
Client/Service YMCA of Greater Toronto/service organization
Type Franklin Gothic Deepdene
Ink Black and four match colors on white
Printing Offset

Concept Even though this 1993/94 annual report features match colors, the designers chose black-and-white halftones to create a friendly, inexpensive feel that matches the charitable organization. Unusually, the designers chose to use black-and-white photography even on color pages. Clever diagrams and charts enliven the short section of financial data at the back.

Design Strategy The lack of emphasis on color begins with the black-and-white cover. Right-hand pages are for text, varying type size and style but always black on white. Left-hand pages are for photographs—alternating full-page black-and-white shots with black-and-white cutouts on green or yellow pages. Duotones add a hint of color but maintain the look of black and white.

YMCA
of Greater Toronto

Annual Report 1993/94
(and picture book)

All ages, all stages. Who is a YMCA participant? Chances are, someone (in fact, many someones) you know. In Greater Toronto, 178,000 people — enough to fill the SkyDome three times over and have people hanging from the rafters and overflowing into the aisles, as well. They are new immigrants and fourth generation Canadians. All ages, all stages of ability. Some can afford to give generously to our YMCA, others are having a tough time and could not participate without financial assistance. They are ALL welcome.

Recipe for Growth and Development

1. Take a group of people who are on Unemployment Insurance or Social Assistance.

2. Add some dedicated YMCA staff, such as:
   Two top-notch chefs
   An employment counsellor
   A food service co-ordinator

3. Mix in a lot of training in hospitality which includes à la carte cooking skills and dining room service skills.

4. Add a dollop of lifeskills training. Mix carefully for 30 weeks until independence, self-esteem and hospitality skills rise to the top.

5. Invite everyone — *we mean everyone* — to come and enjoy the results at the YMCA Hospitality Training Program Restaurant!

Say YES to better job prospects!

You may have heard about them. You may even know them. Dropouts. Laid-off workers. Those who have never held a job longer than a few weeks. Educated people from foreign countries unable to get a job because employers are afraid to take a chance — unable to see their worth. People who need to upgrade their skills. Students in need of challenging summer work programs. People down so long, they are unable to hold their heads up. Older workers trying to get back into a tough work force. Budding entrepreneurs eager to start their own small businesses. People who are trying to learn English as a second language. People who can't read or write in any language. These are the 10,000 people who have used YMCA Employment & Training programs this past year.

Age Distribution of YMCA Participants

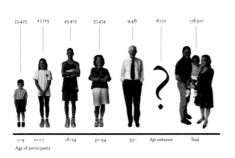

0-9	10-17	18-29	30-54	55+	Age unknown	Total
33,425	27,725	43,423	57,474	9,481	6,772	178,300

Age of participants

Distribution of Volunteers

Total: 8,063

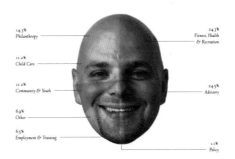

14.3% Philanthropy
11.2% Child Care
11.2% Community & Youth
6.9% Other
6.5% Employment & Training

24.3% Fitness, Health & Recreation
24.5% Advisory
1.1% Policy

Kwasha Lipton

Art Director/Studio Toni Schowalter/
Toni Schowalter Design
Designers/Studio Toni Schowalter,
Martin Perrin/Toni Schowalter
Design
Photographer Brad Martin
Client/Service Kwasha Lipton/
employee benefits consulting
Paper Gilbert Esse Cover, White,
Smooth Finish; Ikonofix Cover,
Matte, Recycled
Type Franklin Gothic, Letter Gothic
Ink Black and match gray on white;
bright purple
Printing Offset
Software QuarkXPress

Concept For "Who We Are and
What We Do," a capabilities
brochure for an employee benefits
consulting firm, the designers created
an engaging piece that emphasized
the firm's personality. Not inexpensive (it features die-cut sleeves and
duotone photographs), the brochure
uses black and white to communicate
friendliness rather than to meet a budget. The white cover is backed with
bright purple for contrast.
Design Strategy This copy-heavy
brochure keeps potential clients reading by breaking the main body of the
rectangular piece into two small
squares and interspersing the business
copy with friendly photographs and
amusing quotations. The copy simu-
lates something typed rather than
designed, and the quotations are each
given a different design treatment.
The effect is of being in a room full
of interesting, friendly and caring
people.
Print Run 20,000

CSA Archive

Art Director/Studio Charles Anderson/Charles S. Anderson Design Co.

Design Directors Charles Anderson, Joel Templin/Charles S. Anderson Design Co.

Designers/Studio Joel Templin, Paul Howalt/Charles S. Anderson Design Co.

Client/Product CSA Archive/stock illustration

Type Cg Alpine Gothic/Prestige Elite

Ink Black

Printing Pad/screenprinting

Software Aldus FreeHand

Concept Packaging design for this compact disc and its holder emphasizes simplicity, in contrast with the compact disc's myriad contents: 100 line images, 80 dingbats, 100 sounds and quick-time movies. Instead of the typical plastic jewel case, a tin canister—chosen for its industrial feel—holds the disc.

Special Production Technique In the studio's trademark fashion, the canisters were sandblasted to a dull finish, pad printed, embossed and individually numbered.

Print Run 3,000

Gilbert Paper

Art Director/Studio John Sayles/
Sayles Graphic Design
Designer/Studio John Sayles/Sayles
Graphic Design
Client/Product Gilbert Paper/paper
Paper Gilbert Oxford
Type Various, including hand-
rendered
Ink Black on gray
Printing Offset
Software None

Concept The theme "One by One"
set the tone for this promotion distributed to paper merchants and designers. One designer created the entire
piece, using one color of ink. Inside
the custom-printed box are a puzzle, a
booklet, a die-cut tray and a keychain.
The booklet emphasizes the design
possibilities of using one ink color,
both full-strength and in dot screens.
The dynamic imagery includes race
cars and motorcyclists, playing on the
pun "won" by "one." Color is provided only by the green paper laminated
to the tray and the plastic keychain
that "binds" the booklet.

Special Production Techniques This
labor-intensive project was assembled
by hand. The box and jigsaw puzzle
were printed on text-weight paper and
then laminated to chipboard.
Print Run 30,000

Steve Niedorf

Art Director/Studio Joel Templin/
Templin Design
Designer/Studio Joel Templin/
Templin Design
Client/Service Steve Niedorf/
photographer
Paper Kraft
Type Memphis, Futura, Clarendon
Ink Black and white on Kraft
Printing Offset
Software Aldus FreeHand

Concept Instead of working with
one of his client's photographs, the
designer chose to represent his business with a playful black-and-white
illustration. Kraft paper was an inexpensive choice for this budget system,
which is enhanced by the paper's
weight and by large blocks of solid
black and white.

Special Printing Techniques The
envelopes and the backs of the business cards are black, while the fronts
of the letterhead and envelope flaps
are white. A double-hit of white
ensured even, opaque coverage.

Norcen Energy Resources

Art Director/Studio Kit Hinrichs/
Pentagram Design, Inc., San
Francisco

Designer/Studio Piper Murakami/
Pentagram Design, Inc., San
Francisco

Photographer Jeff Corwin

Illustrators Max Seabaugh (maps),
Helene Moore

Client/Service Norcen Energy
Resources/diversified natural
resources enterprise

Paper Potlatch Vintage Gloss
(cover), Sundance Vellum Bright
White

Ink Black, spot and full varnish, and
match colors on white

Printing Offset

Concept Compelling black-and-
white halftones are the heart of the
design for this annual report. They
give the highly diversified and techni-
cal company a human face. Dense
pages of text, which highlight the
company's global activities and
financial performance, are brightened
by spot color (in tables, figures and
callouts), illustrations and maps.

Design Strategy The central section,
printed in black and white on coated
paper and further brightened with
varnish, depicts industrial equipment
and people at work. Short, dynamic
captions in sans serif type explain
what the company does by describing
its employees at work.

NORCEN ANNUAL REPORT 1991

RESOURCE DEVELOPERS

Wildcat blowouts showering black rain are part of the lore from the industry's romantic past. A gambler's hunch rewarded by the fortunes of chance. Today, oil finds are anything but blind luck. Recovering hydrocarbons from the earth is a carefully calculated business, requiring ingenuity, documented research, scientific interpretation and economic savvy. Frontier wildcats are more the exception than the rule. Engineer-ing acumen focuses on maximizing existing assets by tapping the full potential of known reserves. Sophisticated geophysical instruments are helping to discover new reservoirs in old oil fields, and enhanced recovery methods are extending the productive life of operating wells.

LIKE FILLING IN A PICTURE BETWEEN THE DOTS, THE EXPLOITATION TEAM EXAMINES WELL DATA AND CORE SAMPLES FROM EXISTING OIL FIELDS TO FORM ASSUMPTIONS ABOUT WHETHER MORE DEPOSITS LIE BEYOND THE EDGES OF POOLS OR BETWEEN EXISTING WELLS.

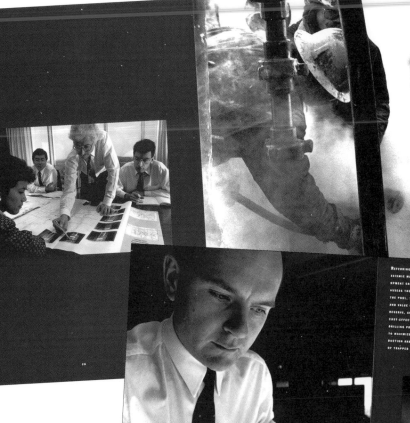

REFERRING TO 3-D SEISMIC MAPS, DEVELOPMENT ENGINEERS ASSESS THE SIZE OF THE POOL, TYPE AND VALUE OF THE RESERVE, AND MOST COST-EFFECTIVE DRILLING PROGRAM TO MAXIMIZE PRODUCTION AND RECOVERY OF TRAPPED OIL.

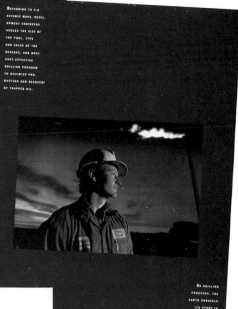

AS DRILLING PROCEEDS, THE EARTH UNRAVELS ITS STORY IN LAYER UPON LAYER — A DRAMA THAT SPANS BILLIONS OF YEARS AND PROVIDES CLUES TO THE ORIGIN AND EVOLUTION OF LIFE ON THE PLANET.

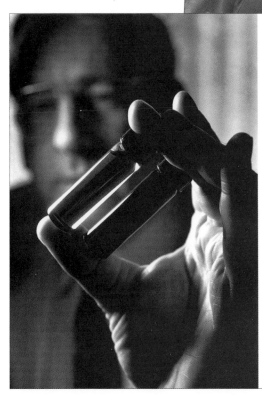

IMPROVED WELL COMPLETION TECHNIQUES HELP EXTRACT MORE OIL BY DISSOLVING OR FRACTURING ROCK FORMATIONS TO ENHANCE PERMEABILITY SO HYDROCARBONS CAN FLOW MORE FREELY TO THE SURFACE.

ENGINEERS MONITOR EACH OPERATING WELL SITE THROUGHOUT ITS PRODUCING YEARS, DEVELOPING UPDATED PRODUCTION STRATEGIES TO OPTIMIZE RECOVERY AND EXTEND THE ECONOMIC VALUE OF THE RESERVE.

In Situ

Art Director/Studio David Betz/
D. Betz Design
Designer/Studio David Betz/D. Betz
Design
Client/Service in situ/art gallery
Type Matrix Wide, Palatino
Ink Black-and-white vinyl on black-
and-white nylon
Software Adobe Illustrator

Concept Although one of the most
readable color combinations, black
and white is rarely used for signage.
Here, it was an aesthetic choice rather
than a practical one. The client wanted a neutral, modern design to match
his interiors, a choice that would
allow colorful artwork to be dis-
played to best advantage.
Special Production Techniques For
a storefront gallery on a street of old
shops, a banner extending over the
street gives the door maximum exposure. Durable nylon fabric with
computer-cut vinyl lettering is an
inexpensive, easily produced solution.
Cost $250 (production)

International Rectifier

Design Studio Point Zero
Photographer Bill Vanscoy
Client/Service International Rectifier/
industrial manufacture and supply
Paper Potlatch Quintessence Dull
Cover and Text, Proterra Natural
White
Type Bodoni, Berthold Regular
Ink Black, match gray, and metallic
inks on white
Printing Offset
Software Adobe Illustrator,
QuarkXPress

Concept This annual report showcases colored papers and metallic inks
within its unpretentious black-and-
white cover. The cover image represents the company's staple business:
semiconductor component manufac-
turing and supply. Inside, duotones of
similar subjects, printed with metallic
inks and dull gray, complement the
businesslike text, presented in match
gray on heavily coated white stock.

Malofilm

Art Directors/Studio Diti Katona,
John Pylypczak/Concrete Design
Communications Inc.
Designer/Studio Renata Chubb/
Concrete Design Communications
Inc.
Photographer Bernard Bohn
Client/Service Malofilm/entertain-
ment
Paper Supreme
Type Bembo, Bell, Centennial
Ink Black and match gray on white
and off-white
Printing Offset

Concept A match greenish gray gives
warmth to this dynamic annual report
for an entertainment company. Extensive use of photographs, reproduced
as tritones for maximum effect, con-
tributes to the exciting mood of this
piece.
Special Visual Techniques Much of
the text is presented in white type
reversed out of dense black-and-
white photographs. This unusual
treatment works because the type is
arranged in readable chunks, and is
interspersed with longer text in traditional black on white. While the text
is more challenging to read, financial
data is straightforward: black with
gray headlines on light gray, uncoated
paper.
Print Run 100,000

HOME VIDEO

Malofilm holds exclusive distribution agreements with
Canadian, American and foreign distributors and studios
such as Paramount Pictures, Turner Home Entertainment,
Trimark and Republic Entertainment. We release films on
home video for the rental market, generally six months
after their theatrical run is over, however some films are
produced for release directly to video. We also market
titles from our world renowned library of films and
television programs to the sell-through market, where
consumers purchase instead of rent videocassettes. We
design the video jackets, posters, ads, point-of-sale and
other promotional material, implement marketing campaigns and arrange for the duplication, packaging and
shipping of videocassettes to wholesalers who in-turn supply our product to local video rental stores and chains such
as Blockbuster and Rogers. In the sell-through market,
we sell to rackjobbers who in turn supply retailers such
as Price Club, IGA and Sam the Record Man. Our sales are
based on firm orders, thus keeping inventory to a mini-
mum. We usually take a commission or pay royalties to
our suppliers once prepaid amounts are recouped.

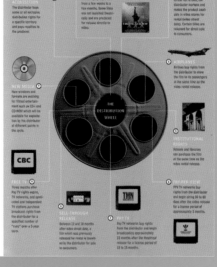

Harvey Hess

Art Director Philip Fass

Designer Philip Fass

Client/Service Harvey Hess/music criticism and college instruction

Paper Nekoosa offset card stock

Type Aurea Inline, Commercial Script, Franklin Gothic Heavy and Book, Helvetica Condensed

Ink Black on white

Printing Xerography

Software QuarkXPress, Aldus FreeHand

Concept The client holds regular house concerts to generate interest in the arts and in a local arts agency that brings classical music ensembles to the community. Invited guests include people from all walks of life and from all income levels. On a tight budget, the designer used multiple pieces, text in French and a hand-tied binding to create an invitation that recipients would enjoy reading, would keep and would remember.

Special Visual Effect A band of fluorescent orange paper, sealed with a simple white circular sticker, complements the elegant black-and-white piece.

Cost $150

Print Run 200

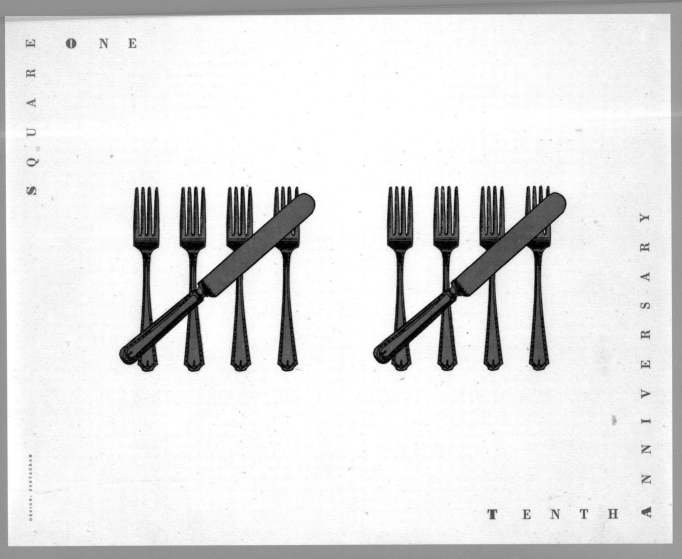

SQUARE ONE

ANNIVERSARY

TENTH A

DESIGN · PENTAGRAM

Square One

Art Director/Studio Kit Hinrichs/
Pentagram Design, Inc., San
Francisco
Designer/Studio Lisa Miller/
Pentagram Design, Inc., San
Francisco
Client/Service Square One/restaurant
Paper Simpson Equinox
Ink Black and metallic silver on
white
Printing Offset

Concept This clever poster uses spare
type and an old engraving to great
effect. The size of a place mat (and
heavy enough to use as one), it
announces a restaurant's tenth
anniversary with wry, understated
wit.

98181

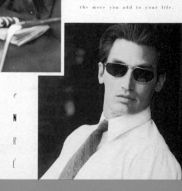

98181

IT WANTS FOR EXPLANATION.
IT DEMANDS INVESTIGATION.
WHAT IS THIS CURIOUS ENUMERATION?
TOMORROW WILL TELL. BUT TODAY OFFERS
ONLY THEORIES AND QUERIES—SOME TRULY
HEARD, SOME JUST IMAGINED, ALL WITH HINTS.
1. A NEW EXHIBIT AT THE SEATTLE ART MUSEUM? *(Not, but there could be a connection.)* **2.** A NEW LOTTERY GAME? *(98181 is the opposite of a gamble.)* **3.** SPORTSWRITERS' CONSENSUS ON THE YEAR OF THE SEAHAWKS' FIRST SUPER BOWL WIN? *(Shows you how little sportswriters know.)* **4.** ANOTHER TV SHOW ABOUT HIGH SCHOOL? *(98181 is more elementary and more advanced.)* **5.** AVERAGE DAILY TEMPERATURE IN YOU-KNOW-WHERE? *(98181 is hot, but not that hot.)* **6.** A NEW MOVIE? *(In our wildest dreams.)* **7.** A NEW NIGHTCLUB? *(Now there's an idea.)* **8.** A NEW STORE? *(Why would anyone name a store 98181?)* **9.** A NEW BANK? *(Yeah, sure, and the code to its vault; help yourself!)* **10.** THE AMOUNT YOU WIN IF YOU GUESS CORRECTLY? *(Sorry, everyone wins on this one, even if you don't have a clue.)*

UNTIL TOMORROW, 98181 REMAINS A VERY LARGE MYSTERY.

Bon Marche

Creative Director/Studio Robert Valentine/Valentine Group
Designer/Studio Dina D'ell Archiprete/ Valentine Group
Photographer J.R. Duran (fashion photos)
Client/Service Bon Marche/retail store

Concept This comprehensive advertising campaign for the opening of a flagship store in Seattle included newspaper and magazine ads, billboards, bus ads, shopping bags and other collateral. To build interest in the new store, the designers began the campaign with teaser ads featuring the store's ZIP code, which no other building shared, in black over photos of the building's architectural details.

Design Strategy Black and white gives the architectural shots weight and dignity, displaying the intricate stone carvings with timeless elegance. It also ties the many pieces together and differentiates them from typical large ad campaigns, which are usually done in color.

Blackhawk Grille

Art Director/Studio Rick Tharp/
THARP DID IT
Designers/Studio Kim Tomlinson,
Jean Mogannam, Rick Tharp/
THARP DID IT
Client/Service California Cafe
Restaurant Corp./restaurateurs
Type Hand-lettered
Software None

Concept Not a traditional choice for
signage, black fit this project because
of its name (Blackhawk Grille) and
because black was used extensively
in the interior design. Silver substi-
tutes for gray or white. The letters
and custom door handles were made
of powder-coated aluminum. The
bolo tie was made of sterling silver,
to match the aluminum door and sign.

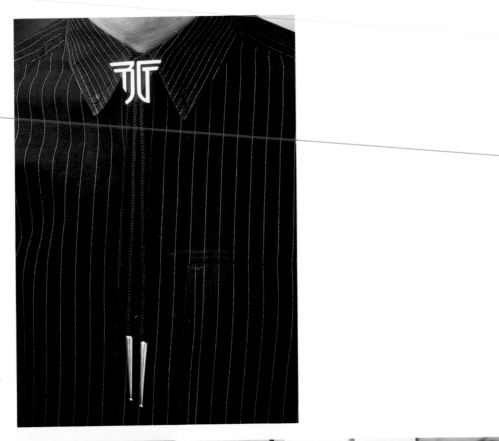

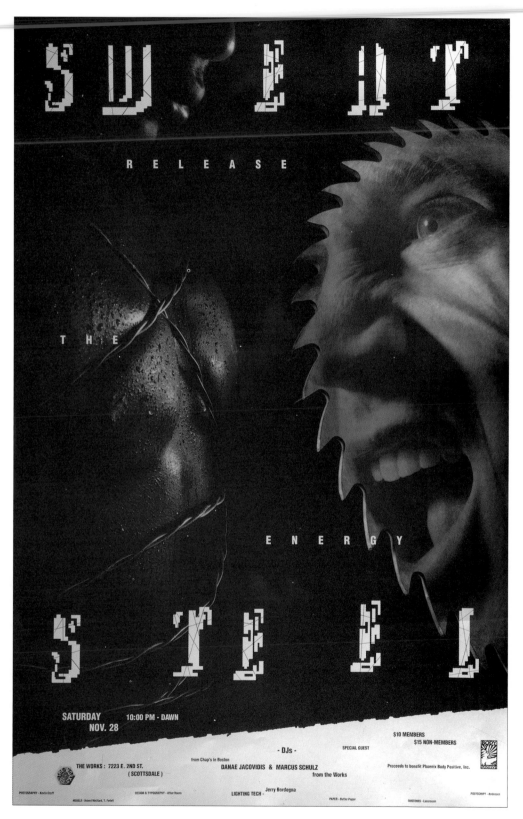

Sweat and Steel

Art Director/Studio Russ Haan/After Hours Creative

Designer/Studio Todd Fedell/After Hours Creative

Photographer Kevin Cruff

Client/Service Phoenix Body Positive/early intervention programs for people with HIV

Paper Consolidated Productolith

Type Helvetica Condensed Bold, Custom

Ink Black and gray/metallic mix on white

Printing Offset

Software Adobe Illustrator

Concept This poster for a fund-raiser at a techno-industrial nightclub uses powerful images to communicate the event's name, "Sweat and Steel." A custom mix of gray and metallic silver inks helped give the piece a steel-like finish that reinforced the photographs and the hard-edged, industrial look. The image was also reproduced on postcards.

Cost Donated

Print Run 1,000

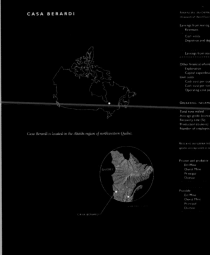

TVX Gold

Art Directors/Studio John Pylypczak, Diti Katona/Concrete Design Communications Inc.

Designer/Studio Scott A. Christie/Concrete Design Communications Inc.

Photographer Deborah Samuel

Illustrator Tom Hunt

Client/Service TVX Gold/mining company

Paper Scheufelen Phoenix Imperiel

Type Gill Scala

Ink Black, match grays and green on white

Printing Offset

Concept Black-and-white photographs give this annual report for a mining company a detached, almost dreamlike mood. Reproduced as tri-tones, the photographs are exceptionally dimensional, and their lack of true white gives them a dusty, murky feel.

Text and Financial Data The opening text pages, half black on white and half white on black, use light green as an accent color. Straightforward and crisp, they are all business. Financial data, presented in black with green titles on white, uncoated stock, are equally efficient. Only the cover and the central nine pages of photographs separating the text from the financial data break the pattern, inserting a strong but mysterious personality.

The $550 million plant is among the most modern in the world and ➤
employs state-of-the-art technology throughout.

The operation employs 11 of these 120 ton trucks to move over 50,000 tons of material daily.

Part of the 16,500 ton per day plant including the eight leaching tanks.

The volcanic rock that contains the ore is at times ➤
porous and mostly oxidized.

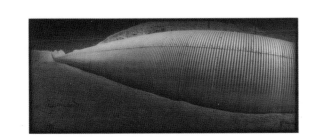

Tailings are transported 1.3 kilometres via covered conveyor system to the disposal area.

Water is pumped at a rate of 70 litres per second. This salt lake is located 40 kilometres from the plant.

HOW Magazine

Art Directors/Studio Scott Finke,
Laurel Harper/*HOW* Magazine
Designer/Studio Rick Tharp/THARP
DID IT
Client/Service *HOW* Magazine/
graphic design magazine
Ink Black on white
Printing Offset
Software None

Concept Rather than making it
inconspicuous, the designer integrated the magazine's UPC bar code with
his design for the cover. It's printed at
an angle, disguised as a classical column. Though unorthodox, an angled
bar code is readable by electronic
scanning equipment as long as the
lines are straight and vertical.

₇0 89484 01000 0₁

48236 52050

UPC Bar Codes

Art Director/Studio Rick Tharp/
THARP DID IT
Designers/Studio Karen Nomura,
Jana Heer, Laurie Okamura, Rick
Tharp/THARP DID IT
Client/Service Rentsch Tool
Supplies/retailer; Sebastiani
Vineyards/vintner; Studio Magic/
video products
Ink Black
Software None

Concept Although bar codes are now
a necessary part of packaging, the art
director of this project doesn't believe
that they have to be boring. These
three UPC bar codes, designed to
complement their product and package designs, are readable by any
scanner. The trick is space and ink.
Design elements are placed outside of
the scannable area or in ink colors
scanners cannot read.

0 88232 42032 2

Etaoin Shrdlu

Art Director/Studio Nan Goggin/
University of Illinois at Urbana-
Champaign
Designers/Studio Fred Daab, Brian
Curry, Gregg Snyder, Nan Goggin,
Mark Fetkewicz, Elizabeth Postmus,
Paula Curran, Christina Nordholm,
Jeff Clift, Fanky Chak, Vince Parker,
Joe Kukella, Chris Waegner/
University of Illinois at Urbana-
Champaign
Paper Cross Pointe Halopaque Blue-
White, Text
Type Baskerville, various
Ink Black on white (text); white on
black (cover)
Printing Hand-printed on a Universal
I Vandercook Press

Concept A collaborative book project
by a professor and graduate students,
this book gets its name
from the way printers
once marked a line of
type to be discarded: by
running a finger down
the first line of a Linotype
keyboard. A theme, sleep
and sleep cycles, unifies
the book through short
copy on the left-hand
pages. Each designer cre-
ated one right-hand page.
The designers printed and
produced the book them-
selves, which allowed some
to add color to their pages
with rubber stamps or tip-
ins.
Print Run 150

'etaoin shrdlu'

A night of sleep usually consists of four to six such cycles. With each subsequent cycle, delta sleep gets shorter and the REM period lengthens. During the last cycle, REM sleep can last for 30 to 60 minutes.

Rose,
oh reiner Widerspruch
Lust,
Niemandes Schlaf zu sein
unter soviel
Lidern.

The first Day's Night had come —
And grateful that a thing
So terrible — had been endured —
I told my Soul to sing —

She said her Strings were snapt —
Her Bow — to Atoms blown —
And so to mend her — gave me work
Until another Morn —

And then — a Day as huge
As Yesterdays in pairs,
Unrolled its horror in my face —
Until it blocked my eyes —

My Brain — began to laugh —
I mumbled — like a fool —
And tho' 'tis Years ago — that Day —
My Brain keeps giggling — still.

And Something's odd — within —
That person that I was —
And this One — do not feel the same —
Could it be Madness — this !

We can only speculate about one of the most striking cognitive aspects of dreams: that is, the failure to remember most of them. In dreaming, the brain-mind follows the instructions: "integrate all signals received into the most meaningful story possible; however farcical the result, believe it; and then forget it." The "forget" instruction is most simply explained as the absence of a "remember" instruction. *I can't remember if it was a nightmare or reality... I just hope I never have to go through that...again.* **Even though the content of each dream is highly personalized, the form of dreaming is shown to be analogous to organic** *Why does the eye see a thing more clearly in dreams then the mind while awake?* **dementia with its visual hallucinations, its disorientation, its confabulation, and its memory loss.**

The cyclic nature of the sleep-wake cycle has been associated with activity in specific areas of the brain and with the release of chemicals that influence sleeping and waking.

PAST

I

kept dreaming that

I was in Shanghai

in 1915

with someone

I didn't know

Now I keep dreaming

I was killed there

that I am with

the same person

in Paris in 1992

Tomorrow

I leave for Paris

LIFE

Figure 6.7 shows these changing sleep patterns.

PACIFIC MOUNTAIN CENTRAL

2:45AM LAKELAND, GEORGIA 1971. I'M SEVEN AGAIN, BUT I LOOK AND FEEL LIKE I'M TWENTY EIGHT.

2:57AM I'M HOME, MOM AND DAD ARE FINE. I REMEMBER... ANY MORE.

3:37AM FLYING OVER THE AGUHUS 09 SEA

5:20AM I DON'T KNOW WHERE I AM

I LAY DOWN AFTER A LONG DAY. MY MIND IS TIRED AND MY BODY IS WEAK. SOON MY SUBCONSCIOUS WILL TAKE OVER AND TAKE ME PLACES THAT SEEM TO BE OUT OF REACH. I WONDER WHERE IT WILL TAKE ME TONIGHT?

Some people believe that if a person dreams he can fly, he has repressed sexual desires. If that is true, I'm in deep trouble. Dreams might be windows to the past. In a previous life I could have been a bird, a plane or even Superman.

Studies of Christiana

Art Director/Studio Steve Ditko/CFD
Design

Designers/Studio Steve Ditko, Mike
Campbell/CFD Design

Photographer Rick Rusing

Illustrator Luis Tomás

Client/Product Uh, Oh Clothing
Boutique/clothes

Paper Neenah Environment, Desert
Storm Wove; Consolidated
Productolith

Type Bodoni, hand-lettering

Ink Black on unbleached

Printing Waterless printing, dryography process

Software None

Concept This provocative direct-mail
piece—all black but with tipped-in
four-color photographs—masquerades as an artist's sketchbook and
tells the story of his doomed affair
with the beautiful but untamed
Christiana. The twelve-page book is
filled with his pen-and-ink sketches,
diary notes and color photographs of
Christiana, which are stuck on the
pages with masking tape. Complete
with smudges, fingerprints, worn
edges and even flowers pressed
between a spread, the convincing
piece shows fewer clothes than a
traditional catalogue, but is far more
compelling.

Cost $35,000

Print Run 3,500

Art Directors Club of Indiana

Art Director/Studio Eric Kass/Eric Kass Design

Designer/Studio Eric Kass/Eric Kass Design

Client/Service The Art Directors Club of Indiana/professional organization

Paper Warren Patina Matte, Neenah UV/Ultra II, Neenah Classic Crest

Type Ocra; Meta Normal, Bold and Caps

Ink Black and metallic silver on white, overall varnish

Printing Offset (brochure and business card), laser (letter, certificate, mailing label)

Software QuarkXPress, Adobe Photoshop

Concept This direct-mail campaign for a professional organization used black and white to unify offset- and laser-printed pieces, and to create a layered, industrial design. A slogan, "you are a link," and the image of a chain run through each piece.

Design Strategy The designer created the chain image by scanning a real chain on a desktop scanner, saving photography fees. On the offset pieces (the brochure/mailer and the membership card), the chain was printed as a duotone in black and silver. The laser-printed pieces look anything but generic. The versatile design translates well to letter and mailing label, while vellum gives the certificate further distinction. A touch of color comes from the red stamp bearing the member number, and the black envelope completes the effect.

Cost Donated

Print Run 1,000 (brochure and business card)

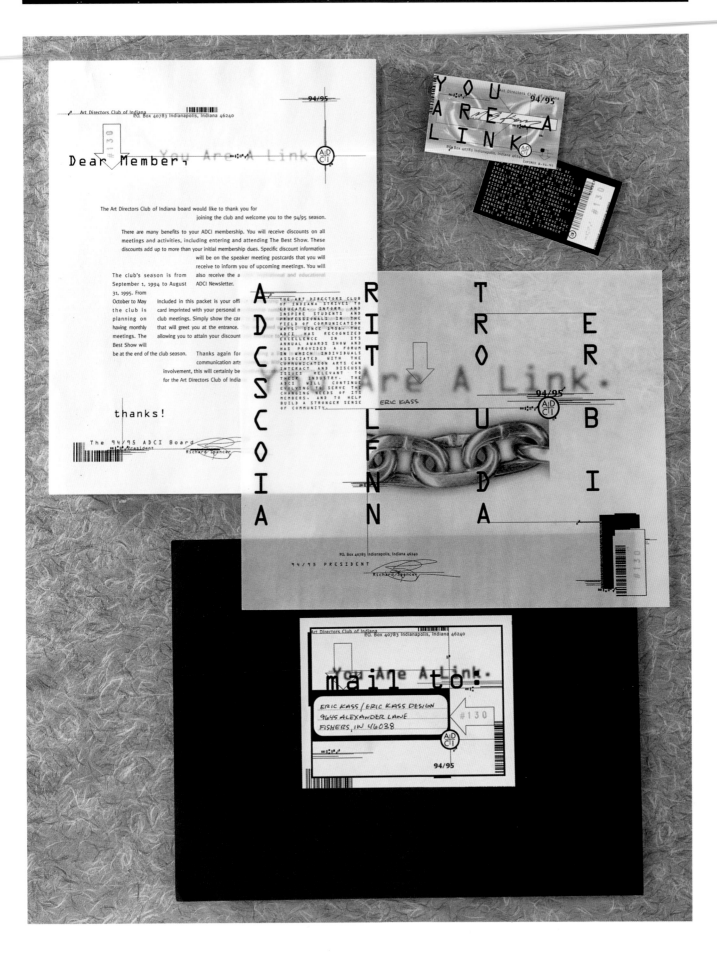

Stanley Rowin Photography

Art Director/Studio Stewart Monderer/Stewart Monderer Design, Inc.

Design Director/Studio Kathleen Smith/Stewart Monderer Design, Inc.

Designer/Studio Kathleen Smith/Stewart Monderer Design, Inc.

Client/Service Stanley Rowin Photography/photography

Paper Gleneagle Dull

Type Gill Sans

Ink Black, match gray and spot varnish on white

Printing Two-color sheet-fed offset

Software QuarkXPress

Concept For this direct-mail promotion for a photographer, the designer showcased photos taken at an elementary school. She capitalized on the match gray used for the duotones and ornamented the tri-fold piece with bars in black, pure gray, and warm brown match gray.

Cost $3,500

Print Run 2,000

This was a great

assignment.

Stanley Rowin's photography is both compelling and very real. He approaches each assignment with an eye for detail while looking for that perfect moment that is a summation of the situation.

Whether it's shooting in the studio for Lipton Tea or capturing children at play at the Pike School, Stanley brings his own special aesthetic to the scenes. If you agree, call him at: (617) 437-0641.

Re: The Pike School. A photo essay on the school to be used for a viewbook.

Stanley Rowin's photography is both compelling and very real. He approaches each assignment with an eye for detail while looking for that perfect moment that is a summation of the situation.

Whether it's shooting in the studio for Lipton Tea or capturing children at play at the Pike School, Stanley brings his own special aesthetic to the scenes. If you agree, call him at: (617) 437-0641.

Photos © Stanley

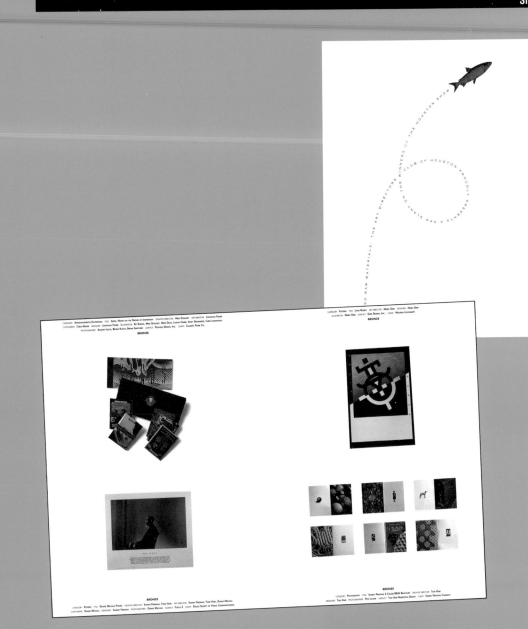

Art Directors Club of Houston

Art Director/Studio Jay Loucks/ Loucks Atalier

Designers/Studio Tad Griffin, Jay Loucks/Loucks Atalier

Client/Service The Art Directors Club of Houston/professional organization

Paper Various

Type Copperplate, Futura

Ink Black and silver on white and brown; match gold and bronze; four-color process

Printing Offset

Software Adobe Illustrator, Adobe PageMaker

Concept The cover of this show annual, a special issue of the club's quarterly magazine, gains distinction from its black-and-white design. The long title, arranged elegantly on the thick white coated paper, marks the leap of a fish suggested by the show's theme (Not So Raw Materials) and printed in metallic silver.

Special Visual Effects The showbook makes extensive use of color, from the Sunday newspaper comics used as flyleaves to the color pages depicting top winners. But black-and-white pages are also used as accents. Vellum paper, printed with black on both sides to create the illusion of a match gray, marks changes in "chapters," depicting a messy desktop and typical judges' comments. Winners of the bronze awards are reproduced in black and white, punched up with metallic bronze headlines.

Cost Design and printing donated

[T-26]

Art Director/Studio Carlos Segura/
Segura, Inc.

Designer/Studio Carlos Segura/
Segura, Inc.

Illustrator Tony Klassen

Client/Product [T-26]/type

Paper Newsprint

Type Tema Cantante (primary),
various

Ink Black and match gray on white

Printing Offset

Software QuarkXPress, Adobe
Illustrator, Adobe Photoshop

Concept A new digital type foundry
featuring typefaces by contemporary
designers, [T-26] produces catalogs
that are as unusual as their wares.
This one, printed on white newsprint,
features bold layouts that emphasize
the display qualities of the typefaces,
rather than simply showing them in
different sizes. Text qualities are
shown through a variety of interesting quotations or original poetry,
rather than greeked copy.

Design Strategy Match gray used on
the cover and sporadically throughout
the piece enlivens the piece without
destroying its deliberately low-budget
look.

Cost $3,000

Print Run 5,000

PAUL COUVRETTE

PHOTOGRAPHY
54 Florence Street Ottawa, Canada K2P 0W7
Tel: (613) 238-5104 Fax: (613) 234-2214

PAUL COUVRETTE
PHOTOGRAPHY
54 Florence Street Ottawa, Canada K2P 0W7
Tel: (613) 238-5104 Fax: (613) 234-2214

PAUL COUVRETTE PHOTOGRAPHY
430 Gladstone Avenue Ottawa, Canada K2P 0Z1
Tel: (613) 238-5104   Fax: (613) 234-2214

Paul Couvrette

Art Director/Studio Terry Laurenzio/
246 Fifth Design
Designer/Studio Sid Lee/246 Fifth
Design
Client/Service Paul Couvrette/
photographer
Paper Fox River Circa Select
Type Helvetica, Futura
Ink Black and foil stamp with tinted
varnish
Printing Offset
Software QuarkXPress

Concept This letterhead for a professional photographer uses black and
white as a subtle reference to the negative and positive images that are part
of a photographer's trade.
Special Printing Technique The back
of each piece, including the envelope,
is printed solid black, with the photographer's name reversed out. On
the front, the name is foil stamped in
a tinted varnish. When held up to the
light, this printing device allows the
photographer's name to glow softly.

Christopher Conerly

Art Director/Studio Christopher Conerly/Art Direction
Designer/Studio Christopher Conerly/Art Direction
Photographer Dave Shafer
Retouching Danny Strickland/ Graphic Center
Client/Service Christopher Conerly/ independent creative director, advertising
Ink Black on white
Printing Offset
Software QuarkXPress, Adobe Photoshop

Concept The designer, an independent advertising creative director, originally planned this design for color printing. He discovered, however, that black and white best communicated the idea behind the design— and was also, of course, less expensive. Though at first concerned about the bleed photo, the designer discovered that it was not a problem for his printer.
Print Run 1,000 (initial)

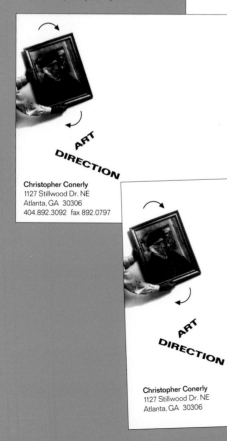

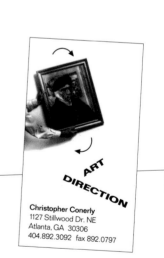

Interior Focus

Art Director/Studio Lynn Springer/
DL Graphics Studio
Designer/Studio Lynn Springer/DL
Graphics Studio
Client/Service Interior Focus/
interior design
Paper Howard Crushed Leaf Cream
Type Poppl-Laudatio Condensed
Ink Black on off-white
Printing Offset
Software Adobe Photoshop, Adobe
PageMaker

Concept While keeping costs down
was paramount to this start-up interior
design firm, it could not afford a low-
budget image. The designer used a
speckled paper, a rich antique textile
design and a screen tint to create an
upscale look using only black printing. The textile image, ghosted to a
pale gray, makes an elegant frame for
the business information.
Cost $655

Cafe Voltaire

Art Directors/Studio Diane Purcell,
Steve Wall/Rock, Paper, Scissors
Designers/Studio Diane Purcell,
Steve Wall/Rock, Paper, Scissors
Photographer Gail Pollard
Client/Service Cafe Voltaire/
vegetarian restaurant
Paper Cross Pointe Genesis Text,
Milkweed
Type Caslon Antique (name),
Akzidenz Grotesk
Ink Black on off-white
Printing Offset
Software QuarkXPress, Adobe
Photoshop

Concept Vegetables are the star of
this letterhead package for a vegetarian
restaurant that also hosts experimental
theater and music performances. The
client's only directive was to use the
paper with the highest recycled paper
content currently available. To capture
the client's intellectual philosophy,
the designers chose to use as orna-
mentation nothing more than simple
photographs of vegetables, made
dramatic by black-and-white printing.
They chose Caslon Antique for the
restaurant's name to recall the Cafe
Voltaire, a hangout for Dadaists at the
end of World War II, and writer/
philosopher Voltaire himself.
Cost $2,500

Café Voltaire
3231 North Clark Street Chicago, IL 60657 312-528-3136
handmade natural foods, theory, manifestoes, poems, pictures, music, performance, coffee

Mark Epstein   Owner

Café Voltaire
3231 North Clark Street Chicago, IL 60657 312-528-3136

Emerson, Wajdowicz Studios, Inc.

Art Director/Studio Jurek Wajdowicz/ Emerson, Wajdowicz Studios, Inc.

Designer/Studio Jurek Wajdowicz/ Emerson, Wajdowicz Studios, Inc.

Client/Service Emerson, Wajdowicz Studios, Inc./graphic design

Paper Simpson Vicksburg Starwhite

Type Helvetica Neue (customized)

Ink Black and match gray on white

Printing Offset

Software QuarkXPress, Adobe Illustrator

Concept The word "hope" shines in this simple New Year's greeting card, printed in black and a deep match gray ornamented by a row of tiny type in white. The somber card was enlivened by a bright red envelope.

Works/San Jose

Designer/Studio Joe Miller/Joe Miller's Studio

Client/Service Works/San Jose/ contemporary art and performance gallery

Paper White index

Type Various

Ink Black on white

Printing Offset

Software QuarkXPress, Pixar Typestry, Adobe Photoshop, Adobe Dimensions, Adobe Illustrator

Concept Used as both mailers and handbills, these pieces announce shows and performances at a contemporary art gallery. Although black and white was a budgetary choice, it works well to unify the pieces, which otherwise share only a distinctive size (4½ x 11). Creative use of type, layout, illustration and photography work with strong design to belie the minuscule budget.

Cost $200 per event (film and printing)

Print Run 2,500 per event

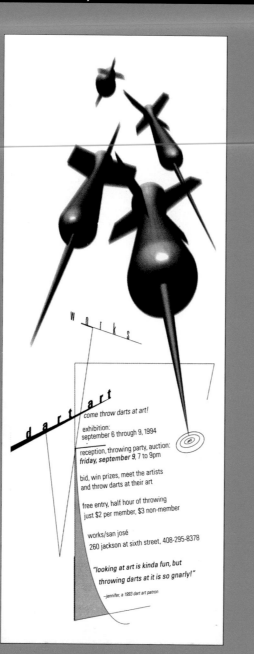

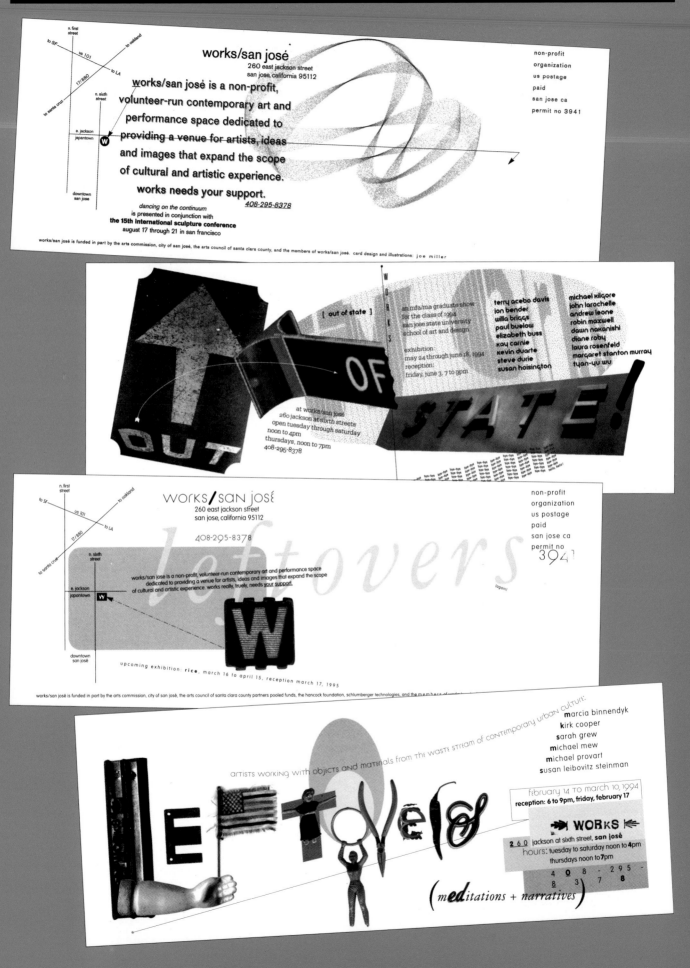

Cleveland Restoration Society

Art Director/Studio Pam Cerio/Pam Cerio Design

Designer/Studio Pam Cerio/Pam Cerio Design

Photographer Don Snyder

Client/Service Cleveland Restoration Society/nonprofit urban development organization

Paper Centura Gloss Cover

Type Univers 65, Bodoni Book

Ink Black on white

Printing Offset

Software QuarkXPress

Concept Good design gives character and interest to this low-budget mailer announcing a public forum on a proposed building, a piece that could easily have been mundane. The ghosted photograph and map place the subject in context, while the black bars with reversed-out type make sure that essential information (the date and title of the forum) isn't missed. The back of the mailer, an all-type treatment, benefits from generous white space and the graphic division of the rectangular card into two squares, one gray and one white.

Cost $1,200 (design, paper donated)

Print Run 6,500

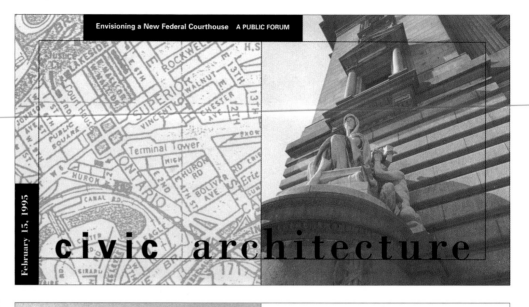

Envisioning a New Federal Courthouse   A PUBLIC FORUM

February 15, 1995

civic architecture

Envisioning a New Federal Courthouse   A PUBLIC FORUM

Please join us as we look at the possibilities for a new Federal Courthouse to be built in downtown Cleveland. A $150 - 200 million project, this structure will contain 800,000 square feet and could be as high as 25 stories. The highly recognized Boston firm, Kallmann, McKinnell & Wood Architects, has been selected to design the building. Cleveland is known for its civic architecture, clustered around the 1903 Group Plan. Clevelanders have an exciting opportunity to play a positive role in the location, design and building of the newest civic building in our city.

Come hear the presentations, contribute your ideas and share your vision!

Wednesday, February 15, 1995
5:30 p.m. - Public Forum, Cash Bar following the Program
Ohio Theatre at Playhouse Square Center, Cleveland, Ohio

IN THIS FORUM WE WILL:
• Look at how Cleveland has planned and implemented civic architecture projects in the past.
• Create a vision for how a Courthouse could contribute to Cleveland's future.
• Look at the reality of civic architecture today in light of the Cleveland project.
• Consider initial design thinking and the possibilities for the new building.

Then we will allow for public input. What do *you* think?

MODERATOR: Joseph D. Roman, Executive Director of Cleveland Tomorrow
PANELISTS WILL INCLUDE: Richard T. Latkowski, Project Manager, General Services Administration; **Michael McKinnell,** Principal, Kallmann, McKinnell & Wood Architects

FOR MORE INFORMATION, PLEASE CALL 621-1498

Cleveland Restoration Society
457 Statler Office Tower
1127 Euclid Avenue
Cleveland, Ohio 44115

This public forum is sponsored by the Cleveland Restoration Society, CSU's Maxine Goodman Levin College of Urban Affairs, the Urban Design Center of Northeastern Ohio, the American Institute of Architects, the Committee for Public Art, and the Cleveland Foundation for Architecture. This forum has been organized with important assistance from Cleveland Tomorrow, Playhouse Square Center, the General Services Administration, and the City of Cleveland.

DESIGN: Pam Cerio   PHOTOGRAPHY: ©1994 Don Snyder

Strangelove Internet Enterprises

Art Director/Studio Terry Laurenzio/ 246 Fifth Design

Designer/Studio Sid Lee/246 Fifth Design

Client/Service Strangelove Internet Enterprises/internet publishing

Paper Beckett Expressions Iceberg

Type Copperplate 31AB

Ink Black on white

Printing Offset

Software QuarkXPress, Adobe Illustrator

Concept For this letterhead for a computer publisher, black and white was a design, not budgetary, choice. The designer used black and white to represent a computer's binary "yes and no" language. The business logo appears in pale gray—actually, a screen of black—to represent the medium allowing users and publishers to communicate.

Special Printing Technique The back of each sheet is printed in black, double-hit for maximum density, with the logo and circle at the bottom of the page reversed out for added graphic impact.

Cost $8,000 (letterhead, second sheet, business card, #10 envelope and 10 x 13 envelope)

STRANGELOVE INTERNET ENTERPRISES INC.
SIE@STRANGELOVE.COM

208 SOMERSET STREET EAST, SUITE A OTTAWA, ON CANADA K1N 6V2
TEL: 613.565.0982 FAX: 613.569.4433

JOHN CURTIN.SEXBOY
STRANGELOVE INTERNET ENTERPRISES INC.
208 SOMERSET STREET EAST, SUITE A
OTTAWA, ON CANADA K1N 6V2
TEL: 613.565.0982 FAX: 613.569.4433
CURTIN@STRANGELOVE.COM

NATALIE STRANGELOVE . HEAD HONCHO
STRANGELOVE INTERNET ENTERPRISES INC.
208 SOMERSET STREET EAST, SUITE A
OTTAWA, ON CANADA K1N 6V2
TEL: 613.565.0982 FAX: 613.569.4433
SIE@STRANGELOVE.COM

California Harvest Ranch Market

Art Director/Studio Mark Sackett/ Sackett Design Associates

Designers/Studio Mark Sackett, Wayne Sakamoto/Sackett Design Associates

Illustrators Mark Sackett, Wayne Sakamoto

Client/Product California Harvest Ranch Market/organic food

Paper Neenah Fiber Added Terrazzo, Wove Finish

Type Hand-drawn, typewriter

Ink Black on off-white

Printing Offset

Concept The client, an organic food market operator, wanted black-and-white letterhead to communicate a rough, unpretentious look. The designer created the identity, reminiscent of old-fashioned food crate design, then "deteriorated" it by enlarging and reducing it several times on a photocopier. The similarly distressed type treatment matches the rustic look of the logo and the textured paper.

Cost $2,000 (including packaging)

Print Run 500

**Setting your sights
on higher visibility.**

It's that time of year. The time to start planning for a successful NeoCon'92. This year, NeoCon features new dates, dramatically increased educational programs and events, an integrated, aggressive marketing campaign, and dynamic new promotional opportunities. It's all designed to ensure the most successful NeoCon ever.

There are several new ways to keep a high profile throughout NeoCon92. Beyond promoting your special events in the official NeoCon program, you can sponsor some of the many NeoCon programs or receptions.

→ furnish your m

NeoCon92

NeoCon92

NeoCon92

check all that apply

Sponsoring a speaker, special event or incentive

Publishing details of our special events in the official NeoCon Directory

Advertising in the NeoCon Directory

Mailing lists for the NeoCon Program Brochure

PLEASE CONTACT US

REGARDING THE

NeoCon

OPPORTUNITIES AND

PROGRAMS LISTED.

Mail this form, or fax it to the NeoCon office at 312.527.7782. Or call 312.527.7552

NAME

TITLE

COMPANY

ADDRESS

CITY   STATE   ZIP

TELEPHONE

FAX

furnish your mind.

NeoCon92

NeoCon 92

Art Director/Studio Carlos Segura/
Segura, Inc.
Designer/Studio Carlos Segura/
Segura, Inc.
Client/Service Chicago Merchandise
Mart/NeoCon 92 Conference
Type Letter Gothic, various
Ink Black on off-white
Printing Offset
Software QuarkXPress

Concept Produced on a budget, this
mailer uses "low-budget" images as
part of its design statement. One of
many pieces produced for a conference on workplace planning and
design, it went to tenants of the mart,
explaining how the conference would
work and how to best promote their
showrooms.
Design Strategy A simple grid and
type treatment unifies all seven
pieces, which are ornamented by photographs and borders that emulate
those composed of old-fashioned line
tape. The main copy is presented in a
sleek modern typeface, while addi-
tional messages appear in faces that
can be found on typewriters.
Print Run 2,000

Hinge

Designers/Studio Jilly Simons, David Shields/Concrete®

Client/Service Hinge/recording studio

Paper Mead Mark V

Type Letter Gothic, Cochin, Trade Gothic, Swiss 721, Gill Sans, Fette Fraktur

Ink Black and varnish on white

Printing Offset

Software Adobe Illustrator

Concept For these cards, used for thank-you notes and reply cards, the designers used "black space" to great advantage. Black was the predominant color in the client's corporate identity, and so a natural choice for these cards. Dynamic type treatment and bars and curves that recall sound waves stand out against the dense black ink. The contrast is further emphasized by an overall varnish.

Cost $800

Print Run 750 per card

Hartmarx

Art Director/Studio Carlos Segura/
Segura, Inc.

Designer/Studio Carlos Segura/
Segura, Inc.

Client/Product Hartmarx/clothing

Paper Wyndstone (cover)

Type Beowulf

Ink Black, gold and varnish on off-
white

Printing Offset

Software QuarkXPress

Concept Designed to introduce Karl
Lagerfeld's autumn 1994 collection
of menswear to retailers, this piece
features three papers: a thick, pebble-
finished cover stock; a white, striped
vellum flyleaf; and heavy, off-white
coated paper for the striking photographs.

Design Strategy The designer
matched the piece to the photography provided by the client. The suits
are shot at provocative angles and
shown on unusual mannequins—the
clothing designer himself is the only
person pictured. The modern typeface takes on a classic air in this
design, which, though produced on a
budget, has the look and feel of an
expensive dinner jacket.

Print Run 1,500

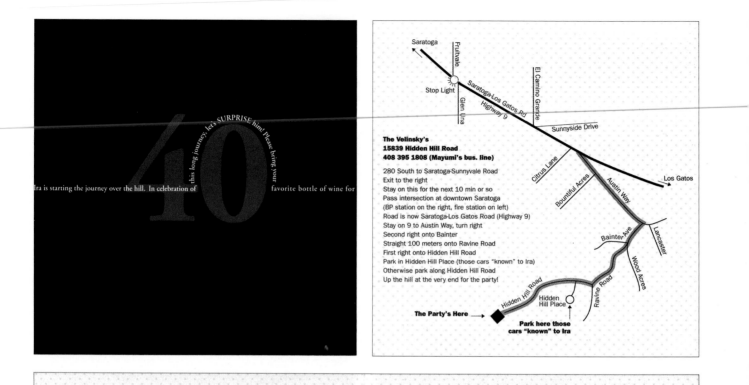

Ira is starting the journey over the hill. In celebration of this long journey, let's SURPRISE him! Please bring your favorite bottle of wine for

The Velinsky's
15839 Hidden Hill Road
408 395 1808 (Mayumi's bus. line)

280 South to Saratoga-Sunnyvale Road
Exit to the right
Stay on this for the next 10 min or so
Pass intersection at downtown Saratoga
(BP station on the right, fire station on left)
Road is now Saratoga-Los Gatos Road (Highway 9)
Stay on 9 to Austin Way, turn right
Second right onto Bainter
Straight 100 meters onto Ravine Road
First right onto Hidden Hill Road
Park in Hidden Hill Place (those cars "known" to Ira)
Otherwise park along Hidden Hill Road
Up the hill at the very end for the party!

The Party's Here

Park here those cars "known" to Ira

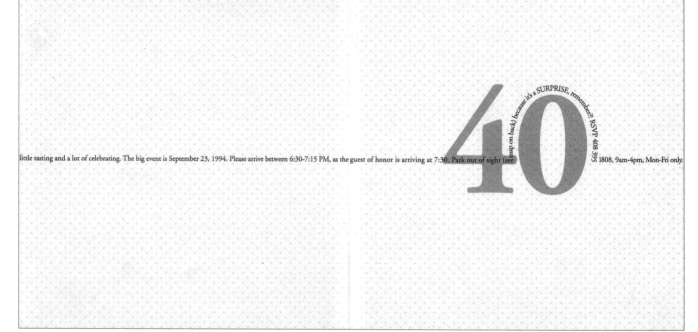

little tasting and a lot of celebrating. The big event is September 23, 1994. Please arrive between 6:30-7:15 PM, as the guest of honor is arriving at 7:30. Park out of sight (see map on back) because it's a SURPRISE, remember? RSVP 408 395 1808, 9am-4pm, Mon-Fri only.

Fortieth Birthday Invitation

Art Director/Studio Jodie Stowe/ Stowe Design
Designer/Studio Jodie Stowe/Stowe Design
Paper Strathmore Elements, Dots
Type Garamond, Helvetica
Ink Black on white
Printing Offset
Software Adobe Illustrator

Concept A small budget and a big birthday were the reasons the designer used black and white for an invitation to a friend's surprise party. A line of small type runs across the face and inside of the card, making an elegant loop over the zero in the number 40, which is the most prominent design element. White reverse type, a gray screen tint and patterned paper give a pleasing variety to this simple piece.

Print Run 50

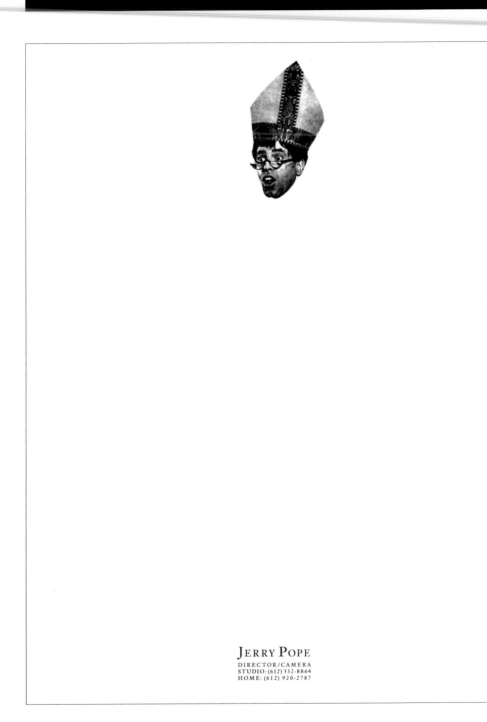

JERRY POPE
DIRECTOR/CAMERA
STUDIO: (612) 332-8864
HOME: (612) 920-2787

Jerry Pope

Art Director/Studio Bob Barrie/Fallon McElligott

Designer/Studio Bob Barrie/Fallon McElligott

Client/Service Jerry Pope/television production

Paper Beckett Text

Ink Black on ivory

Printing Offset

Software None

Concept The client's name was all the direction needed for this piece. Its humor and charm lie partly in the crudity of the illustration, produced with a craft knife and a photocopier. The photograph of Jerry Lewis is from his film *The Nutty Professor.*

Print Run 2,000

Advertisements

Perhaps the most common use of black-and-white design is for advertisements. Some media, such as newspapers, all but demand it. In others, such as four-color magazines, black-and-white ads are the only ones some clients can afford.

Good ad designers are adept in using black and white. The ads in local and national newspapers and in magazines of all types and circulations are an endless source of design ideas. There you'll find new and different ways to use type, photos, illustration and copy to sell a product in a crowded marketplace. And there you'll find an ever-changing record of what works, as well as what doesn't work.

The ads on the following pages demonstrate that, if you have a strong idea, you really don't need color to convey it effectively. But note that you do need good copy and superior visuals to convey your idea; when either one of these elements is weak, an ad won't work.

YMCA

Art Director/Studio Jac Coverdale/
Clarity Coverdale Fury Advertising,
Inc.
Photographers Jim Hubbard, Steve
Umland
Copywriter Jerry Fury
Client/Service YMCA/service orga-
nization
Type Cochin
Ink Black on white
Software QuarkXPress

Concept For this pro bono project,
designers created public service
announcements to be distributed to
two thousand YMCAs around the
country, for use in local newspapers
and other publications. Through dramatic photographs and short, hard-
hitting copy, the PSAs show how
important the YMCA's programs for
low-income families are to the recipients, especially children.
Cost Pro bono

We're not the only youth organization actively recruiting new members.

Today, gangs are a growing problem in cities across the country.
That's why the YMCA is so important.
Each year, the Y in our community helps give kids the positive
experiences and healthy role models they need to resist drugs, gangs,
crime and violence.
So help kids make their mark in society the right way.
Support the place that supports kids and families. **The YMCA Y**

When you live in a place like this, camping in a tent isn't exactly roughing it.

The fact is, 1 out of 3 kids under 18 live in poverty. Which means a
lot of kids are growing up without some of life's basic necessities.
That's why the YMCA provides programs for kids who otherwise
might not get the positive experiences and caring adult attention they
need. Help us make life better for those who have it rough.
Support the place that supports kids and families. **The YMCA Y**

Q101

Art Director/Studio Carlos Segura/
Segura, Inc.
Designers/Studio Carlos Segura, Vito
Costarella/Segura, Inc.
Illustrator Vito Costarella
Client/Service Q101/radio station
Type Resbaloso
Software QuarkXPress, Adobe
Photoshop

Concept One of four designed to be
printed in the *Chicago Reader*, this
full-page newspaper ad for a radio
station depends on an attention-
grabbing illustration and a brief catch
line. The station's call letters are not
emphasized—instead, the illustration
communicates the type of music it
plays and the type of people who lis-
ten to it.
Design Technique The design for the
figure's body is based on a crushed
box of Marlboro cigarettes.

Jeremiah's

Art Director/Studio Joe Paprocki/
Fallon McElligott
Copywriter Dean Buckhorn
Illustrator Joe Paprocki
Client/Service Jeremiah's/record
store
Type Hand-rendered
Software None

Concept Produced on a minuscule
budget, these ads for a music store
ran in a college newspaper. Created
and assembled entirely by hand, they
capture the look and irreverent humor
of the audience. The asymmetrical
shape of the ads further helped them
stand out.

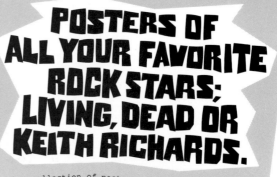

IT'S A WATER HEATER. IT'S A FURNACE. IF IT WERE A PERSON, IT WOULD BE IN THERAPY.

Furnace   *Water Heater*   *CompleteHeat*

It's called CompleteHeat. And it's very well-adjusted. First of all, it's a high-efficiency furnace. It's also a high-efficiency water heater with a virtually unlimited supply of hot water. Combine all that with 100 years of Lennox experience and you have to be crazy not to sell it. For more information, call 1-800-515-4736.   **LENNOX**

Lennox Industries

Art Director/Studio Holland Henton/ GSD&M Advertising

Design Directors/Studio Holland Henton, David Crawford/GSD&M Advertising

Designers/Studio Holland Henton, Jason Shaw/GSD&M Advertising

Illustrator Ozzie Buckler

Client/Service Lennox Industries/ heating and cooling

Type Magnesium, Antique Roman

Software Adobe Illustrator, QuarkXPress

Concept This trade ad for a new high-efficiency furnace/water heater combo uses old-fashioned type, illustration and layout to emphasize the company's hundred-year-old reputation for quality. The graded border, which creates the illusion of a frame, symbolizes heat dissipating from a furnace. Despite the ad's classic look, there's nothing behind-the-times about its catchy copy.

Texas Junk Company

Art Director/Studio Penny Morrison/
Morrison Design & Advertising
Photographer Frank Golden
Client/Service Texas Junk Company/
resale shop
Type Various
Software QuarkXPress

Concept These selections from three
series of newspaper ads for the Texas
Junk Company feature intriguing
photos and generous use of white
space. The designer used a photographer experienced in black-and-white
work to ensure good halftones and
quality photos that didn't need computer alteration.

Design Strategy All ads feature the
store owner because the agency
believes that people spend more when
they're familiar with a store's owner.
The owner, who has worked with the
agency for fourteen years, found that,
once ads with his picture began running, customers began talking to him
as if they knew him.

Cost $2,900

No,
I'm
not
a rock
star.

I'm a junk dealer!
**Texas Junk
Company**
*215 Welch at Taft
Houston 524-6257*

Recycling

Texas
Junk
Co.
524-6257

before it was cool.

But please
don't bring
cans over
here.
215 Welch

Cool Junk.

Texas
Junk
Co.

It's a resale
shop, man.
215 Welch
524-6257

Asche & Spencer

Art Director/Studio Bob Barrie/Fallon
McElligott
Designer/Studio Bob Barrie/Fallon
McElligott
Copywriter Jarl Olsen
Photography Blackbox Stock
Photography
Client/Service Asche & Spencer/
music production
Type Hand-rendered
Software None

Concept This ad, which ran in magazines for advertising creatives and
television producers, grabs attention
with its unusual image, which grows
odder with each viewing. The designer altered the vintage photograph only
once, and with deliberate crudeness,
as if the musical note had been added
to the page with a black pen. The lack
of copy—only a slogan, a name and a
phone number—makes the ad more
intriguing by forcing the reader to call
for more information.
Cost $1,000 (production)

MUSIC YOU CAN'T IGNORE.

Asche & Spencer
FOR A REEL, CALL CAMILLE BENOIT
AT 612·338·4322.

Mothers Against Drunk Driving

Art Director/Studio Randy Hughes/ Clarity Coverdale Fury Advertising, Inc.

Copywriter Bill Johnson

Photographer Curtis Johnson/Arndt

Client/Service Mothers Against Drunk Driving/nonprofit organization

Type Franklin Gothic

Printing Black and tinted varnish on white

Software QuarkXPress

Concept This advertisement, also used as a poster, uses black and white for budget reasons. A tinted varnish helps dull the photograph and give it depth at the same time, while giving the tag line reversed out of the black background more visibility and greater importance.

Design Strategy Like most campaigns aiming to change behavior, this one relies on shock value to make the viewer reevaluate his or her actions. The common phrase "idiot light" takes on a new meaning when paired with the message against drinking and driving.

Cost $2,000 (design donated)

Print Run 2,500

See's

Art Directors/Studio Chris Chaffin, Jennifer Martin/Hal Riney & Partners

Designers/Studio Chris Chaffin (all), Bob Pullum (Father's Day), Jennifer Martin (Secretaries Day)/Hal Riney & Partners

Photographers Hunter Freeman (Father's Day), Will Mosgrove (Secretaries Day)

Illustrators Cynthia Torp (Mother's Day, St. Patrick's Day), Charlie Mize (Secretaries Day)

Client/Product See's Famous Old Time Candy/candy

Type Isadora, Cooper Old Style, Cooper Italic, Metropolis Bold

Concept These newspaper advertisements for a candy company communicate the client's sense of whimsy, and match the candy store's black-and-white decor. Signature candies—chocolate ties for Father's Day, chocolate potatoes for St. Patrick's Day—are highlighted in the vertical ads, while the square ads set a mood with old-fashioned photos and layouts. A distinctive checkered border catches the eye and unifies the ad campaign.

Special Production Technique For the St. Patrick's Day ad, the art director converted airbrush illustrations to heliographs to improve their reproduction.

Russet Potato.

White Potato.

Red Potato.

Sweet Potato.

Sweeter Potato.

In the royal family of tubers, none quite compares to See's fabled Irish potato. Consider its noble attributes: Divinity and English walnuts, pure milk chocolate, cinnamon and cocoa powder. All crowned by three pignolia nuts. (For a wee measure of good luck.) St. Patrick's day is March 17. So remember, "by the piece or by the pound" no one matches See's quality at See's price. After all, who else but the leprechauns at See's could turn a common potato into an unburied treasure?

See's
Famous Old Time Candies

(actual size)

The only tie guaranteed to shrink.

While there's nothing we know of that will prevent the See's Milk Chocolate Father's Day Tie from getting smaller, something tells us Dad will appreciate it all the same. It is, after all, full-sized, Windsor-knotted and, as you can see, inordinately natty. It comes in its own tie box and costs only $6.00.* Sunday the 19th is coming soon so shop early while supplies last. For shop locations and mail orders, call 1-800-347-7337.

See's
Famous Old Time Candies

She changed you. She bathed you.
She wiped your nose.
Somebody give that woman a truffle.

Considering all the icky things moms have to put up with, simply saying "thank-you" on Mother's Day probably isn't thanks enough.

This is where the truffle idea comes in. And well, (as luck would have it) our timing seems to be very good here because we've just finished making one especially for Mother's Day. It's made with real Granny Smith apples, cinnamon and dipped in a white cocoa butter coating. Appropriately, we call it Mom's Apple Pie™ Truffle.

Odds are, however, one just won't do. No sir. So, for a trifle under six dollars, we've made it very easy to buy a half pound of Mom's Apple Pie™ Truffles, neatly wrapped in a real mom-pleasing

Mom's Apple Pie™ Truffles taste like a bite-sized slice of fresh apple pie.

box. This half pound idea, we think, would really tickle her.

Either way, "by the piece or by the pound,"™ no one matches See's quality at See's price. We hope you'll stop by your nearest See's location and buy some. As a matter of fact, we'd venture a guess your Mom is at home right now hoping that's just what you'll do, too. Although there's a chance we could be wrong on that.

For shop locations and mail orders, call 1-800-347-7337.

Famous

It's time again to honor those
who run this country.
That's right, it's Secretaries Day.

John Morgan calls his secretary, "the second most important person in the company." (The first, he says, is his boss's secretary.) And Nina Rowe says that her secretaries are "the glue that holds this business together. Not to mention the mortar, brick and steel."

Well, with Secretaries Day coming up on Wednesday, April 27, we figured John, Nina and a whole lot of others could use a few suggestions on how to show their obvious appreciation.

Like our See's Gold Fancy box. It's a 1-lb. assortment of our popular nuts, chews, creams and other tasty morsels, wrapped in gold and topped with a crisp white ribbon.

The See's Gold Fancy box. A pound of the tastiest decisions your secretary will ever make.

Or, if you'd prefer, give your secretary a gift certificate so he or she can pick out his or her own favorite candies. You'll find that "by the piece or by the pound,"™ no one matches See's quality at See's price.

Of course, once here, you'll also find that we don't have anything quite as extravagant as a ticker tape parade, but then, have you ever known a secretary who would allow such a mess?

For shop locations and mail orders, call 1-800-347-7337.

See's
Famous Old Time Candies

[T-26]

Art Director/Studio Carlos Segura/
Segura, Inc.

Designer/Studio Carlos Segura/
Segura, Inc.

Client/Product [T-26]/type

Type Various

Ink Black on white

Software Adobe Photoshop,
QuarkXPress, Kodak Photo CD,
Adobe Illustrator

Concept This ad, which appeared in
a newsprint magazine, uses screen
tints of black to provide the illusion
of a third color. The digital design,
including layered elements in pure
black and white as well as in gray, is
targeted at the new type foundry's hip
audience.

Design Strategy The target audience
is bound to appreciate the flip attitude
implied by "hiding" the phone number by blurring it, an effect canceled
out by the number's place as the central, and largest, design element.

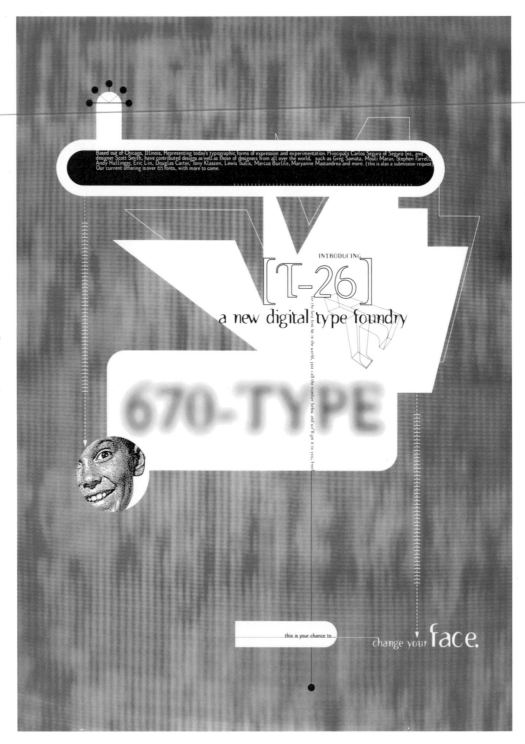

Time Magazine

Art Director/Studio Ellen Steinberg/
Fallon McElligott
Designer/Studio Ellen Steinberg/
Fallon McElligott
Copywriters Bruce Bildsten, Luke
Sullivan, Phil Hanft
Client/Service *Time* magazine/
weekly news magazine
Type New Baskerville
Software QuarkXPress

Concept The designer used black and
white to its best advantage on these
two full-page newspaper ads. The
"Peace Sign" ad delegates the magazine cover to the bottom right corner,
leaving most of the page white except
for four simple drawings that economically communicate the dramatic
shift from war to peace in four countries. Color would have distracted
readers from the message. For the ad
for *Time* on-line, the agency used fin-
gers to create realistic smudges.

Quick. Name a soft drink.

Coca-Cola Co.

Art Director/Studio Bob Barrie/Fallon
McElligott
Designer/Studio Bob Barrie/Fallon
McElligott
Client/Product Coca-Cola Co./soft
drinks
Software None

Concept This black-and-white ad, a
teaser reintroducing Coca-Cola's
classic bottle shape, ran on billboards
in major cities. The silhouette once
again proved its near-universal recognition, and the image was so popular
with Coca-Cola that it used a photograph of one of the billboards on the
cover of its 1994 annual report without any other identifying headline or
copy.
Cost $3,000 (production)

{ADD ONE MORE NUMBER TO YOUR LITTLE BLACK BOOK}
·

458-AIDS
AIDS SERVICES OF AUSTIN

AIDS Services of Austin

Art Director/Studio Brent Ladd/
GSD&M Advertising
Designer/Studio Brent Ladd/
GSD&M Advertising
Photographer Tony Pearce
Client/Service AIDS Services of
Austin/nonprofit organization
Software QuarkXPress

Concept This advertisement, which
appeared in *Sports Illustrated* and
Newsweek, uses a simple message
and design to communicate something few people want to read.
Because of a limited budget, black
and white was a given. But the medium also created an ideal solution, the
"little black book" of ill repute. For
this image, color would have been
superfluous.
Cost Pro bono

Lotus Carpets

Design Studio Design!

Photographer Geof Kern

Client/Service Lotus Carpets/carpet sales

Type Cochin, Letter Gothic

Ink Black on white

Software Aldus FreeHand

Concept These magazine advertisements feature humorous photographs of a utilitarian product. Wry captions add to the sense of the unexpected, while short copy floating on an expanse of black draws attention and showcases the company name.

Design Strategy Budget was the primary reason for choosing black and white, but that choice allows the ads to show the carpet itself, rather than any of the many colors the client sells.

Harlan Saperstein

Art Director/Studio Bob Barrie/
Fallon McElligott
Designer/Studio Bob Barrie/Fallon
McElligott
Copywriter Jarl Olsen
Client/Service Harlan Saperstein/
voice talent
Ink Black and varnish on white
Printing Offset
Software None

Concept The designer created six
images featuring the client's bald
head. They ran as ads in a Minneapolis advertising publication, and
were also printed on card stock and
used as self-promotional postcards.
Black and white made the photographs more striking, and was also
more affordable for the client, who
put a new spin on the old "face for
radio" gag.
Cost $5,000
Print Run 1,000 each of 6 cards

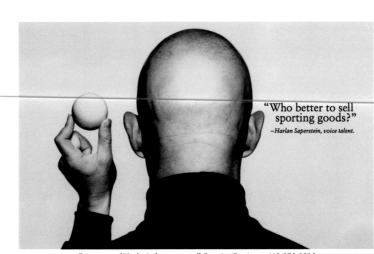

For a copy of Harlan's demo tape call Creative Casting at 612-375-0525.

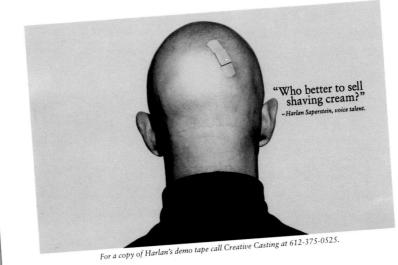

For a copy of Harlan's demo tape call Creative Casting at 612-375-0525.

For a copy of Harlan's demo tape call Creative Casting at 612-375-0525.

For a copy of Harlan's demo tape call Creative Casting at 612-375-0525.

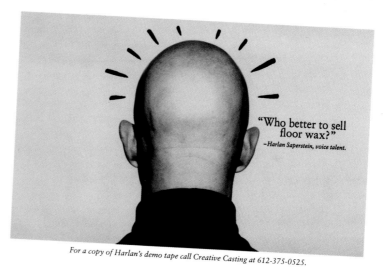

For a copy of Harlan's demo tape call Creative Casting at 612-375-0525.

For a copy of Harlan's demo tape call Creative Casting at 612-375-0525.

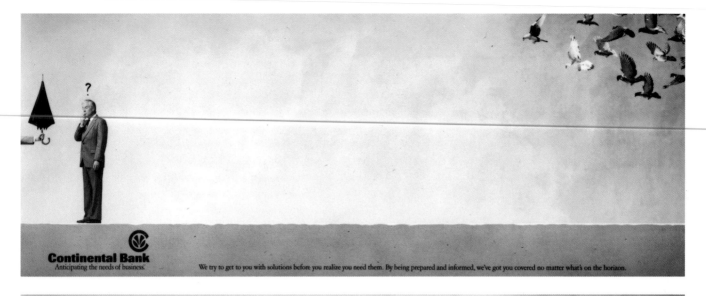

Continental Bank

Art Director/Studio Bob Barrie/Fallon
McElligott
Designer/Studio Bob Barrie/Fallon
McElligott
Copywriter Mike Gibbs
Photographer Rick Dublin
Client/Service Continental Bank/
bank
Type Garamond

Concept To run in major financial
newspapers, the original color version of this magazine ad campaign
for a bank had to be redone in black
and white and resized to fit across
the bottom half of a newspaper
spread. The larger size and mass add
distinction to the campaign, which
features unexpected combinations of
images and copy with punch.

Special Production Techniques
Photographs of the "customers," the
"disasters" and the backgrounds
were all shot separately, then digital-
ly stripped together and retouched.
Cost $100,000 (production, color
and black and white)

When you anticipate as much as we do, you sometimes yourself get ahead of.

CHILDREN NEEDED FOR EXPERIMENTS

Bring your kids to the Austin Children's Museum. They'll get to act like little scientists so they can learn more about the world around them. (No lab coat required)

472-2499

**Austin Children's
Museum**

Art Director/Studio Brent Ladd/
GSD&M Advertising
Designer/Studio Brent Ladd/
GSD&M Advertising
Client/Service Austin Children's
Museum/museum
Software QuarkXPress

Concept Created as a classified ad
for internal museum publications and
for newspapers, this all-type treatment relies on clever copy and a
block of solid black to catch the
reader's attention.
Cost Donated

Your company has a mainframe at headquarters and computers in the branch offices. Plus a phone system. Your customers have computers. And your key suppliers have computers. Yet with all that horsepower in place, how come you still can't move information around from one place to another?

Well, you can. Call Ameritech. We have a history of designing solutions for a variety of business problems. And with our broad range of communications products and services, we can connect all the systems you need access to; making the information your people need available anywhere, anytime. Perhaps

Basically, we sell the tape.

the best thing we can bring to your company is a new way of looking at your communications. It's no longer just the phone system. Or the computer system. Designed intelligently, your communications system can be forged into a real competitive advantage. Something you have that the other guys don't.

See, to our way of thinking, the much talked-about information highway is a given. What we're talking about here is something more. Welcome to the passing lane on the information highway. To find out how to move your company into it, call 1-800-719-5822, ext. 17.

Ameritech
Your Best Link
To Better Communication

Ameritech

Art Director/Studio Tom Lichtenheld/Fallon McElligott
Copywriter Luke Sullivan
Photographer Buck Holzemer
Client/Service Enhanced Business Services/telecommunications
Type Futura, Century
Software QuarkXPress

Concept Part of a campaign in financial newspapers and trade magazines, this ad for a telecommunications company explains a complex concept in one picture and tag line. Copy in italics elaborates, but never degenerates into techno-speak. While black and white was dictated by the medium, color would not have improved the idea.
Cost $60,000

Body Alarm

Art Director/Studio Margaret
Johnson/Fallon McElligott
Copywriter Sally Hogshead
Photographer John Katz
Client/Service Body Alarm/personal
safety device
Type FF Justlefthand
Software QuarkXPress, Adobe
Photoshop

Concept Like many ads for alarms
and other safety devices, these depend on shock value. However, the
imagery is far from typical. Stock textures used as backgrounds create a
menacing atmosphere, at the same
time acting as effective gray space
for the reversed-out white type. The
product is shown almost as an after-
thought, leaving most of the space to
the disturbing headlines and the
wordless implication that buying the
product would keep the reader from
facing such situations.

HOW TO SCREAM FOR HELP WHILE BEING STRANGLED.

During an attack, most are unable to even cry for help. But with a slight
squeeze, Body Alarm screams louder than you possibly could.

BODY ALARM

SO SIMPLE, YOU CAN USE IT WITH ONE HAND TIED BEHIND YOUR BACK.

Most self-defense products require fancy moves or accurate aim.
But just squeeze Body Alarm, and you'll send out a 130 decibel call for help.

BODY ALARM

Get paid to think up stuff like this.

Some ad agency actually paid a writer and an art director to think up this crazy visual idea for an ad. But coming up with wildly creative solutions to real marketing problems is what advertising is all about. And, after 8 semesters at Art Center, you'll have a good portfolio and a good shot at landing a job in a field that's financially as well as creatively rewarding. Call us at 818-584-5035. Or write to Admissions, Art Center College of Design, 1700 Lida St., Pasadena, CA, 91103.

ArtCenter

Art Center College of Design

Art Director/Studio Joe Paprocki/
Fallon McElligott
Copywriter Luke Sullivan
Photographer Rick Dublin
Client/Service Art Center College of
Design/design school
Type Rockwell Condensed

Concept Because the budget was tight for this series of ads that ran in design magazines, the designer focused on all-type solutions (although he indulged in one photograph and a die-cut edge). Snappy copy is the key to the campaign's success. It has the right blend of irreverence and sales to appeal to the target market, would-be design students.

Lesson #1: always remove the lens cap.

You probably know the basics of taking photographs, but you can build a much broader working foundation and begin to develop your own sense of style during one of our night classes. The next course begins soon. Call 818-584-5023. Or write ACAN, Art Center College of Design, 1700 Lida Street, Pasadena, CA 91103.

ArtCenter at Night

OUR CHILI RECIPE IS SO SECRET, EVEN WE DON'T KNOW WHAT'S IN IT.

Serving the same old thing since 1930.

Texas Tavern, 114 Church Avenue, Roanoke, VA 24011. Phone 342-4825. ©1990.

BEWARE OF DOG.

Serving the same old thing since 1930.

Texas Tavern, 114 Church Avenue, Roanoke, VA 24011. Phone 342-4825. ©1990.

IT'S NOT PRETTY. BUT IT'S 85¢.

Texas Tavern
Serving the same old thing since 1930.

Texas Tavern, 114 Church Avenue, Roanoke, VA 24011. Phone 342-4825. ©1990.

Texas Tavern

Art Director/Studio Bob Barrie/
Fallon McElligott
Designer/Studio Bob Barrie/Fallon
McElligott
Copywriter Luke Sullivan
Photographer Bob Barrie
Illustrator Bob Barrie
Client/Service Texas Tavern/
restaurant

Concept Done on a shoestring
budget, these ads for a Roanoke,
Virginia, diner are not a clever ploy
to make a ritzy place look fashionably
greasy. It really is greasy—eight
stools at the counter, two tables, one
cook, real diner food. The ads, which
ran in a local paper, communicate the
place's attitude: no apologies.
Cost-Saving Techniques The art
director took the photographs himself.
Cost $100 per ad

Whitmire's Fine Jewelry

Art Director/Studio Mark Hughes/
Lord, Dentsu & Partners

Designer/Studio Mark Hughes/Lord,
Dentsu & Partners

Photographer Nicholas Eveleigh

Client/Service Whitmire's Fine
Jewelry/upscale pawn shop

Type Microscan

Ink Black on white

Software QuarkXPress, Adobe
Photoshop

Concept Clever copy is the key to
this series of newspaper advertisements for an upscale pawn shop.
Instead of suggesting that potential
clients might need cash, they describe
humorous scenarios that "turn bad
memories into good money."

Design Strategy Deliberately crude
type reversed out of blocks of solid
black emphasizes the text. Intriguing
halftone photographs of pieces of fine
jewelry illustrate the "stories."

THIS IS HOW MANY SAFETY
REGULATIONS OUR GOVERNMENT
IMPOSES ON THE PRODUCT
THAT KILLS OVER 5,000
AMERICAN CHILDREN A YEAR.

There's not a single federal standard governing the safety of one of the most dangerous products made. It's time for our laws to start protecting children, instead of protecting guns.

CEASE FIRE
Children's Defense Fund and Friends

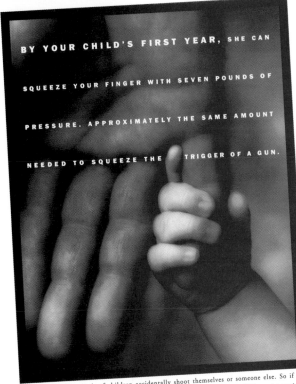

BY YOUR CHILD'S FIRST YEAR, SHE CAN SQUEEZE YOUR FINGER WITH SEVEN POUNDS OF PRESSURE. APPROXIMATELY THE SAME AMOUNT NEEDED TO SQUEEZE THE TRIGGER OF A GUN.

Every year, hundreds of children accidentally shoot themselves or someone else. So if you get a gun to protect your child, what's going to protect your child from the gun?

CEASE FIRE
Children's Defense Fund and Friends

Children's Defense Fund

Art Director/Studio Tom Lichtenheld/ Fallon McElligott
Designer/Studio Tom Lichtenheld/ Fallon McElligott
Copywriter Sally Hogshead
Photographer Buck Holzemer
Client/Service Children's Defense Fund/nonprofit advocacy group
Type Franklin Gothic
Software QuarkXPress, Adobe Photoshop

Concept Provocative images and hard-hitting copy characterize these public service announcements for stricter gun control. Black and white was chosen because it would be less expensive for magazines, which donated space, to print. Pure black bars and frames, used with gray halftones and white type, further dramatize the violent message.

Reelworks

Art Director/Studio Joe Paprocki/
Fallon McElligott
Copywriter Doug de Grood
Client/Service Reelworks/animation
studio
Type Franklin Gothic Medium and
Light

Concept Rather than depicting a car-
toon character, these ads for an animation studio show animation itself.
Simple line drawings reduce animation to its simplest form and demonstrate one of its main uses—depicting
emotion, motion, and senses other
than sight. The ads ran in several
trade magazines and were also used
for a direct-mail campaign.
Design Strategy Not showing examples of the company's work makes
the ads more general. Readers think
of how their work would benefit from
animation, not from a particular style
of animation.

INDICATES SWIFT AND SUDDEN
ACCELERATION OF A PREVIOUSLY
STATIONARY OBJECT OR PERSON.

No one understands animation better than we do. For a copy of our reel featuring
work for clients like Fallon McElligott, Ketchum and MTV, call us at 612-333-5063.   REELWORKS ANIMATION STUDIO

INDICATES INEBRIATION DUE
TO THE OVERCONSUMPTION OF
A FERMENTED BEVERAGE.

No one understands animation better than we do. For our current reel featuring
work for clients like MTV, Hunt/Murray and Fallon McElligott, call 612-333-5063.   REELWORKS ANIMATION STUDIO

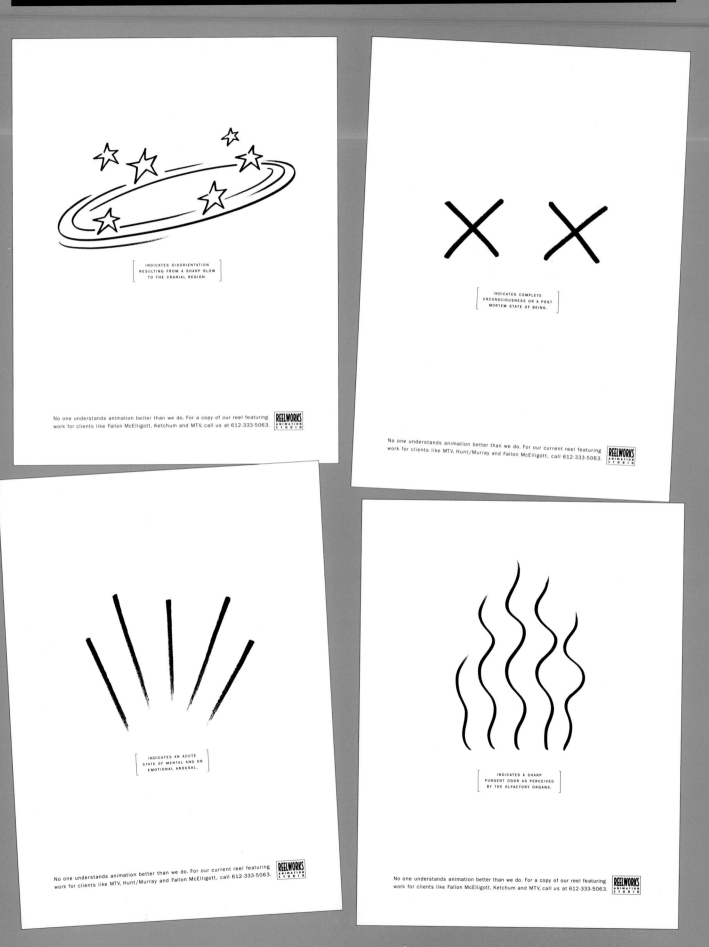

Publications

The following examples show that, contrary to popular belief, black-and-white publications don't have to be less interesting than those produced in color. While black and white was in many cases a budget constraint for the designers who produced these pieces, some chose it for aesthetic reasons. Some with no alternative managed to make a low-budget look into a design statement, while others simply experimented to find the limits of black-and-white design.

This is nowhere more evident than in corporate brochures and annual reports. Sometimes considered the elite projects in graphic design, they can seem to have no real budgets or design parameters. Yet designers who specialize in these deep-pocket projects often choose to include black-and-white spreads in their work, or to work entirely in black and white. Often, this choice is driven by the desire to showcase fine black-and-white photography, usually reproduced as duotones or tritones to improve its resolution. Despite color photography's popularity, black-and-white work still implies a level of quality and artistry that color can sometimes lack. For this reason, it's a natural fit even in the most expensive of designs.

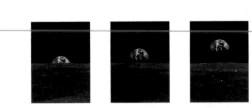

Earth Technology Corporation

Art Director/Studio Lana Rigsby/
Rigsby Design, Inc.
Designers/Studio Lana Rigsby, Troy
S. Ford/Rigsby Design, Inc.
Photographer Gary Faye
Client/Service The Earth Technology
Corporation/environmental, earth
sciences and waste management
consultants
Paper Centura Dull Cover, French
Rayon (financials)
Type Bodoni, Helvetica Black
Extended
Ink Two match blacks, metallic silver
and spot dull varnish on white and
off-white
Printing Offset
Software QuarkXPress

Concept For this annual report, the
designers chose to use black and
white to represent the environmental
consulting firm's strength in reconcil-
ing opposing interests. The clear,
readable text explains this succinctly,
aided by the elegant type treatment
with meaningful—not just decorative—callouts. Lush duotones are
reproduced as both positives and neg-
atives, to repeat the theme.
Text and Financial Data The text,

interspersed with photographs of
nature, is printed on coated stock.
Text appears in silver-gray, black
and white (reversed out of solid
black). Financial information, which
takes up the second half of the piece,
is clearly separated by different
paper and a different type treatment.
Print Run 7,500

GROWTH
vs.
ENVIRONMENT

THE PARADOX OF PROGRESS

THE ENVIRONMENTAL PROTECTION AGENCY PUTS CURRENT COSTS TO REMEDY FEDERALLY REGULATED POLLUTION AT $100 BILLION A YEAR. SINCE GROWTH FUELS POLLUTION, THE TENDENCY'S BEEN TO PIT THE ENVIRONMENT AGAINST PROGRESS. ONE OR THE OTHER. IRONICALLY, AIDING THE ENVIRONMENT SPAWNED GROWTH: $100 BILLION A YEAR IN ENVIRONMENTAL SERVICES. WHILE THIS DOES NOT MEAN THAT $1 SPENT ON THE ENVIRONMENT EQUALS $1 IN EXPANSION, IT SHOWS THAT THE SOLUTION LIES WITHIN THE PROBLEM. THAT'S PROGRESS.

CONFRONTATION
vs.
COLLABORATION

THE CASE FOR COMMON GROUND

IT HAS BEEN ESTIMATED THAT OF $7 BILLION ALLOTTED FOR SUPERFUND CLEANUP IN THE 1980S, NEARLY $5 BILLION WENT FOR LEGAL COSTS. IN SUCH A COMPLEX ARENA LITIGATION IS INEVITABLE, BUT THE GOAL OF REGULATIONS IS TO FIX, NOT CONTEST, THE ENVIRONMENT'S PROBLEMS. TO DATE, LESS THAN 3% OF SUPERFUND WASTE HAS BEEN CLEANED UP. PERCEIVED CONFLICTS OF INTEREST MUST GIVE WAY TO MUTUAL AGENDAS. AFTER ALL, EVERYONE'S IN THIS TOGETHER, INDUSTRY, GOVERNMENT, INDIVIDUALS, INSTITUTIONS — EVEN LAWYERS.

"EARTH...MAY WE NOT INJURE THY VITALS OR THY HEART."
FROM *THE VEDAS* · 3000 B.C.

Merex Corporation

Art Director/Studio Russ Hahn/After
Hours Creative

Designer/Studio Dino Paul/After
Hours Creative

Client/Service Merex Corporation/
employee literacy and math training

Paper Potlatch Quintessence

Type Helvetica, Bodoni, Inserat
Roman

Ink Black on white

Printing Offset

Software Adobe Illustrator

Concept Black and white give maximum punch to this all-type capabilities brochure for a company that
teaches basic literacy and mathemat-
ics skills to workers. The booklet
graphically represents negative atti-
tudes and situations with white type
on black pages and positive respons-
es with black type on white pages.
On the right-hand pages, provocative
comments —"Can't you follow

instructions?"— demonstrate the
company's understanding of their
clients' frustrations and the solutions
Merex offers. Left-hand pages are
used for more in-depth explanations,
presented in classic type arrange-
ments.

Cost $10,000

Print Run 2,500

The THIN MAN

This unfinished *Thin Man* is not merely a first draft of Hammett's last novel. The only apparent connection is that the missing thin man in both is named Wynant, and the name Guild is used for investigators in both.

The protagonist in the novel Hammett published in early 1934 is Nick Charles, an urbane, talkative ex-detective married to a literate woman who is at once sophisticated and naive. (Hammett had, in the period between the two thin men, hooked up with Lillian Hellman. He once told her she was the model for Nick Charles' wife Nora.) In the story at hand the main character is a working investigator — a dark, reticent man named John Guild who reminds us of Hammett's Continental Op. In the 1934 version, set primarily in New York, Guild is a police lieutenant working on the case.

The manuscript of the San Francisco *Thin Man* is 65 neatly typed, double-spaced pages long. Hammett gave away the original in 1942 to be auctioned off in connection with a War Bonds drive. He wrote an explanatory note on this occasion:

"In 1930 I started writing a book entitled *The Thin Man*. By the time I had written these 65 pages my publisher and I agreed that it might be wise to postpone the publication of *The Glass Key* — scheduled for the fall — until the following spring. This meant that *The Thin Man* could not be published until the fall of 1931. So — having plenty of time — I put these 65 pages aside and went to Hollywood for a year. One thing and/or another intervening after that, I didn't return to work on the story until a couple of more years had passed — and then I found it easier, or at least generally more satisfactory, to keep only the basic idea of the plot and otherwise to start anew. Some of the incidents in this original version I later used in *After The Thin Man*, a motion picture sequel. But, except for that and for the use of the characters' names Guild and Wynant, this unfinished manuscript has a clear claim to virginity." The original manuscript is in the E. P. Guyman Jr. Collection, Occidental College, Los Angeles.

BY DASHIELL HAMMETT

1

City of San Francisco

Art Director/Studio Mike Salisbury/ Mike Salisbury Communications Inc.
Designer/Studio Mike Salisbury/ Mike Salisbury Communications Inc.
Client/Service City of San Francisco/ weekly magazine
Paper Newsprint
Type Found
Ink Black on white
Printing Offset

Concept For this opening page of a magazine article, an unfinished story by Dashiell Hammett, the designer chose black and white to help recreate a period feel. A pleasing balance of illustration and type creates interest. The unusual wide column catches the reader's interest, and is not difficult to read for just one page.

Design Strategy Black and white emphasizes the 1940s-style type and old photo by revealing their distinctive forms.

Brookside Capital, Inc.

Art Director/Studio John Bielenberg/
Bielenberg Design

Designers/Studio John Bielenberg,
Allen Ashton, Teri Vasarehlyi/
Bielenberg Design

Client/Service Brookside Capital,
Inc./investment management

Paper Champion Kromekote
Recycled, Gilbert Esse Recycled

Type Gill Sans

Ink Black, match gray and varnish on
white and gray

Printing Offset

Software QuarkXPress

Concept For this brochure, sent to
prospective clients and distributed at
presentations, the designers used
abstract imagery to deliver an understated, elegant feel. Variety is given
to the piece with the use of a number
of different paper stocks: bright
white, coated stock for the outer
pages, matte gray for the inner pages
and a vellum flyleaf. The silver spiral
binding is at once elegant and industrial.

Special Visual Effect The same
image, a photograph of waves, is
used throughout the piece. Printed
with a pearlescent varnish for highlights and a dull match black for the
shadows, it has a different feel from
simple black and white. The inside
cover, flyleaf and matching gray
envelope use the full photo, while the
cover and inside pages break the
wave into squares of various densi-
ties. Simple blocks of text, surrounded by white and gray space, add to
the upscale feel.

Cost $50,000

Print Run 5,000

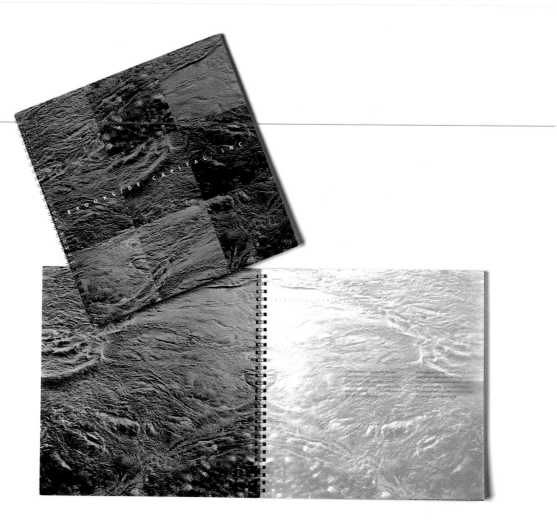

TSL Visuals Group

Art Directors/Studio Mamoru
Shimokochi, Anne Reeves/
Shimokochi/Reeves
Designers/Studio Mamoru
Shimokochi, Nobuo Hirano/
Shimokochi/Reeves
Client/Service TSL Visuals Group/

visual merchandising
Paper Potlatch Quintessence Gloss
Type Bodoni and Bodoni Italic,
Futura Italic and Extra Bold Italic
Ink Black and match gray on white
Printing Offset
Software Adobe Illustrator

Concept This announcement of the
client's new division uses texture,
shape and form to reach a specific
audience: retailers. Copy is reversed
out of the rich textures printed in
black and gray, commanding the
reader's attention. The design is per-
fectly suited to visual merchandising,

a field that relies on texture and
shape to transform empty walls into
retail theater.
Cost $1,500 (printing only)
Print Run 2,000

Pennsylvania State University School of Visual Arts

Art Director/Studio Lanny Sommese/ Sommese Design

Designers/Studio Scott Patt, Brett M. Critchlow/Sommese Design

Client/Service Pennsylvania State University School of Visual Arts/ education

Paper Consolidated Productolith Cover and Text, Dull

Type Various

Ink Black on white

Printing Offset

Software QuarkXPress

Concept Designing this magazine for the sophisticated audience of this scholarly journal, the designers felt free to experiment with type and layout. The magazine was sent to schools, galleries, museums and scholars, and was also sold at the university.

Design Strategy Each article is given a different design treatment, although all share a certain deconstructivist sensibility. Black and white, chosen primarily for budget reasons, adds further continuity and helps assure that even when pushing readability, the designs retained enough contrast to be legible.

Cost $6,000

Print Run 1,500

THE ROMANTIC CONTINUUM

The ever-expanding vortex of Turner's *Hannibal Crossing the Alps* has enveloped 200 years of Romantic convention. The rich tradition established a continuum evident in most succeeding art movements, yielding only to an internal, structural collapse. Today, what remains in the livid air of its passing is the disconcerting void[1] of Friedrich's *Monk by the Sea*.

The Romantic tradition is one of longing. The Romantic strives for a non-secular, spiritual alliance with the universe through a language without ecclesiastical derivation. The language becomes as illusive as the search for cosmic unity. While a strongly established means of expression is difficult to transcend, the institution of a new one becomes unachievable. The Romantics found resolution in modification: the portrayal of natural power persisted but its inclusion of deific or churchly imagery ceased. Nature, once a signifier of Godly power entered the larger realm of the cosmos. Within this context the artist became Christ.

In 1802 the German idealist Schlegel defined beauty as a "symbolical representation of the infinite."[2] The slow and immanent collapse of the symbol during the Romantic age also coincided with the diminished importance of beauty. Edmund Burke's *Philosophical Enquiry into the Origin of Our Ideas of the Sublime and the Beautiful,*[3] of 1757 outlined the characteristics of the sublime in nature, which anchored Romantic thought. He set in motion a polarity to the traditional properties of beauty. According to Burke the sublime possesses the characteristics that traditionally repel beauty such as darkness, immeasurable scale, and all that threatens existence. The sense of beauty remains only as an attractive force. But art no longer had to deal with the appeasement of the eye--only the soul and mind.

It can be argued that the collapse of the symbol in art originates in the Romantics' attempt at universality. Carstens and Blake, artists closely affiliated with that period, searched for an appropriate archetypal language in the private realm of thought and spirit. Their language was esoteric, "obscure in source or interpretation," [4] a language that aspired to be all-inclusive. Rosenblum notes, (though perhaps without full recognition of its importance,) that Piet Mondrian's similar use of the archetypal cross image in his *Circular Composition, Church Facade*. The writer reads the image in a dynamic; it is at once a Christian cross, while also a point of formal convention for centering the work, and, further, the simple [?] this composition of crosses." The multivalence of [?] symbols are seemingly unconstrained to fixed mean [?] at universality make his work at once esoteric and [?]

symbols lost their sacramental worth[5] as they proliferated, the signs of the so-called priests of universality lost their ability to mediate their images.

Linguistics in the Post-Modern age illustrates a tenuous association between words and their signified. Because any symbol, and specifically the symbol of the void, is then rendered complicit, the work of art, as symbol, becomes arguably invalid. The created image is then substantiated entirely by its mere capacity to define art. The void becomes an oppressive presence and the artist's voice all but succumbs to it.

When art is made impotent by the arbitrary quality of visual language, the artist is left only with history, with the supposed expiration of innovation their actions are now determined by a knowing reliance on the past.

There is a common element existing in both Romantic and Post-Modern dis-

---

another other feminism and the prinzhorn collection

The art of the Prinzhorn Collection has held altering positions of privilege and neglect throughout the century, as have the schizophrenic people who helped produce it. The 1922 publication of Hans Prinzhorn's book, *The Artistry of the Mentally Ill,* signalled the peak of the "first wave" of an intense popular fascination with the insane which had been growing steadily since the early 1800's. Romanticism set the tone in its focus on a "search for unprecedented experiences." The search for the new in turn precipitated a preoccupation with the unusual or the abnormal as "manifestations of the unique sensibility."[?] Artists, as well as people in medicine and the newly developed field of psychiatry, (such as Prinzhorn himself), took particular interest in the art of the insane. Most medical and psychiatric studies sought answers to questions regarding, a) the cause(s) of madness and, b) the source(s) of creativity. Often the published research revealed a desire to find a link between (artistic) genius and madness.[?] One author concluded that both artist and madman shared the possession of an unusually large amount of artistic ability and an unusually small amount of reason, the difference being that the genius retained some degree of control over his/her abilities while the insane person did not.[?] It was generally agreed that for the madman (or woman), art was merely a "by-product", that is an accident or quirk of nature. The art of the insane gained status not only because it was a compelling oddity, but also largely due to the uses to which it could be put, both in diagnostic endeavors and as a tool potentially capable of revealing the wellspring of human creativity. The compulsion of these early researchers to seek this wellspring among the insane revealed what became a long lived trend towards viewing the insane as the new *noble savage* who, like the *primitive*, as seen through the eyes of his/her colonizer, was

closer to nature and unfettered by (eurocentric) culture. The insane weren't alone in having this sort of reception; women, children and others (natives such as American Indians) outside the dominant culture were viewed in a similar manner; all were seen as being closer to nature-i.e. lacking a certain part of culture. This conclusion was drawn largely from the Romantic myth of the artist.

The publication of two major volumes on the art of the mentally ill in the early 1920's marked a a small but distinct change in the colonizers mentality apparent in the treatment of the insane. Prinzhorn's book and one by Walter Morgenthaler (*A Mentally Ill Person As Artist,* 1921) both discuss the insane person as artist through the use of the traditional monograph format. The shift from the medical or psychological 'case' to the 'artist', or at least creative person worthy of a monograph, seemed to indicate an increased willingness to view the insane as individuals. Even so, the prevalent tendency was to romanticize the mentally ill. It is doubtful that the "artistry" of the insane would have attained as much public interest if not for the recent appearance of the psychoanalytic theories of Freud and Jung. In light of the former, the insane appeared to have the Id-ent (most "natural" and available) of the Ids, and their art and their illness offered these up for public scrutiny. Jung's concept of archetype also propagated interest. Disillusioned by the war, there was a culture-wide search for renewal and meaning that was focused inward, as the exterior world seemed exhausted. As well, there was a persistent search for new horizons: the art and minds of the insane provided virgin territory for exploration and excavation. Many prominent artists of the time saw the insane as having tapped into a "genuine" creative expression which they sought for themselves. Paul Klee placed the insane in or close to "the

bosom of nature, the primordial source of creation, where the secret key to everything is kept;"[?] Andre Breton is quoted as saying that "art must return to a purely inner prototype or it will cease to exist;" Dubuffet asserted that "madness lightens man and gives him wings."[?] It seems that for[?] artists in the early 20th century, the insane embodied all hopes for the future. By the middle of the century, this connection between the "primordial" mind of the schizophrenic and modern art was used as a tool to discredit art, artists, and contemporary culture. Hitler employed the Prinzhorn collection as proof positive that the artist was basically degenerate and *sick,* a chaotic force capable of undermining civilized culture (read "status quo"). Insane artists had embodied all humankind's worst fears *and* highest hopes, and I suggest that this is typical of the treatment of all "others"; all outsiders.

The current dialogue on the art of the insane focuses heavily on an analysis of the ways in which we have used the insane artist in the past by trying to obtain a clearer understanding of how 'sane' relates to 'insane', how art intersects the two, and how the label on an artist's mental state effects our reception of their work.

The art of the mentally ill has traveled the entire continuum from the Good (high-art, pure-nature, savior of society), through the indifferent (medical symptom, by-product of illness), to the Evil (embodiment of chaos, destroyer of society). There appears to be a lot of effort to "correct" the inclination to romanticize and colonize the insane. But, while there are plenty of assertive claims these days that the insane artist is *artist* first, there is some evidence, especially when examined in the light of certain feminist theories, to suggest that the position held by these artists currently is not radically different from what it was 70 years ago.

I offer the following anecdote as a prelude to the issues of death and dying that will explore in the body of my text. It consists of a three day exercise in "ancestor worship" that I developed for a high school art history class that I taught for twelve years in California. The purpose of such an exercise was to involve students in a realm of inquiry that would enable them to link concepts learned in art history to the big questions that constantly loomed in their minds about their own lives.

During a unit on Roman Art, the concept of "art for the dead" was introduced specifically as it related to the ancestor worship tradition of the ancient Etruscans; the culture whose death masks greatly influenced the honorific portraits of the Romans. In this context, the exercise provided students with opportunities to explore modern counterparts to the Etruscan practice and to identify forms of "death masks" in our century. The Etruscan masks

---

ART in crisis
AN ATTACK ON RECENT BODY METAPHORS

In the early stages of writing this paper, I was faced with three profound issues: ones that required much reflection on my part. They were as follows: first, the national controversy that ensued over censorship in the arts; second, the death of

my father whom I loved dearly; and third, the War in the Gulf. These issues, all dealing with the demise of something significant in my life, were burning in my heart and in my mind. Seeking to gain objectivity in what was an intense personal experi-

ence, I was prompted to write. In doing so, I have attempted to resolve these issues by applying my best sensibilities as an artist and educator; ones that represent a belief in the salvation of the human spirit through artistic expression.

International Typeface Corporation

Art Director/Studio Paul Davis/Paul Davis Studio

Designers/Studio Paul Davis, Lisa Mazur/Paul Davis Studio

Client/Product International Typeface Corporation/type

Paper Newsprint

Type ITC Legacy, Serif and Sans

Ink Black on white

Printing Offset

Concept These spreads from *U&lc* magazine masterfully demonstrate the design possibilities of a new typeface. Switching between typefaces in the same family at every paragraph, the first page describes the typeface's history and designer. The second spread uses quotations to play with letter and layout possibilities, while the last two spreads display the type family in a classic layout.

Design Strategy A magazine devoted to the type its parent sells, *U&lc* is meant to inspire designers to use type well. Each issue contains a feature like this one highlighting a particular face. These features serve as timeless type displays.

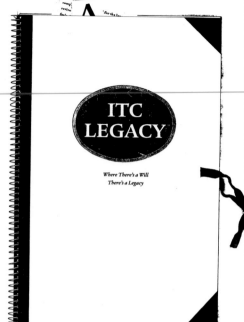

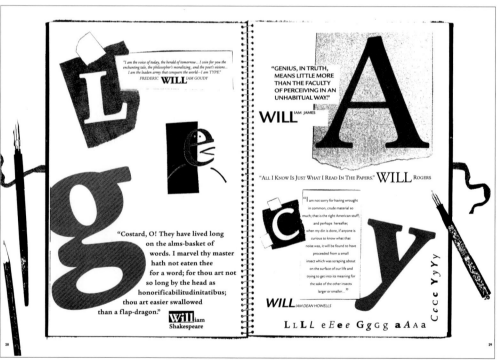

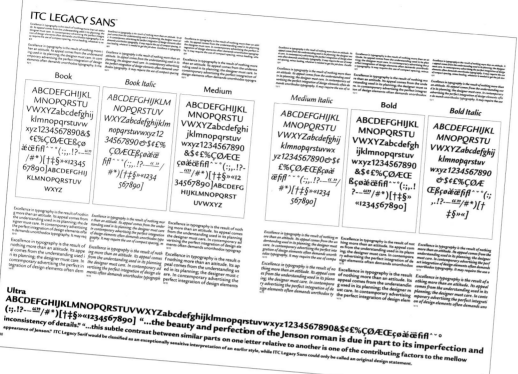

ITC LEGACY SANS™

Book
ABCDEFGHIJKL
MNOPQRSTU
VWXYZabcdefghij
klmnopqrstuvw
xyz1234567890&$
¢£%ÇØÆŒßço
ăœ̆œfifl ˆ ˇ ˚ (:;,.!?-—""
/#*)[†‡§»«12345
67890]ABCDEFGHIJ
KLMNOPQRSTUV
WXYZ

Book Italic
*ABCDEFGHIJKLM
NOPQRSTUV
WXYZabcdefghijklm
nopqrstuvwxyz12
34567890&$¢£%
ÇØÆŒßçoăœ̆œ
fifl ˆ ˇ ˚ (:;,.!?-— ""
/#*)[†‡§»«1234
567890]*

Medium
ABCDEFGHIJKL
MNOPQRSTU
VWXYZabcdefghi
jklmnopqrstuv
wxyz1234567890
&$¢£%ÇØÆŒ
çoăœ̆œfifl ˆ ˇ ˚ (:;,.!?
-—""/#*)[†‡§»«12
34567890]ABCDEFG
HIJKLMNOPQRST
UVWXYZ

Medium Italic
*ABCDEFGHIJKL
MNOPQRSTU
VWXYZabcdefghij
klmnopqrstuvwx
yz1234567890&$
£%ÇØÆŒßço
œ̆œfifl ˆ ˇ ˚ (:;,.!?-—""/
#*)[†‡§»«1234
567890]*

Bold
**ABCDEFGHIJKLM
NOPQRSTU
VWXYZabcdefgh
ijklmnopqrstuv
wxyz1234567890
&$¢£%ÇØÆŒ
ßçoăœ̆œfifl ˆ ˇ ˚ (:;,.!
?-—""/#*)[†‡§»«
«1234567890]**

Bold Italic
***ABCDEFGHIJKL
MNOPQRSTU
VWXYZabcdefghij
klmnopqrstuv
wxyz1234567890
&$¢£%ÇØÆ
Œßçoăœ̆œfifl ˆ ˇ ˚ (:;
,.!?-—""/#*)[†
‡§»«]***

Ultra
**ABCDEFGHIJKLMNOPQRSTUVWXYZabcdefghijklmnopqrstuvwxyz1234567890&$¢£%ÇØÆŒçoăœ̆œfifl ˆ ˇ ˚
(:;.!?-—""/#*)[†‡§»«1234567890] "...the beauty and perfection of the Jenson roman is due in part to its imperfection and
inconsistency of details." "...this subtle contrast between similar parts on one letter relative to another is one of the contributing factors to the mellow
appearance of Jenson." ITC Legacy Serif would be classified as an exceptionally sensitive interpretation of an earlier style, while ITC Legacy Sans could only be called an original design statement.**

ITC LEGACY SERIF™

Book
ABCDEFGHIJKL
MNOPQRSTU
VWXYZabcdefghij
klmnopqrstuvw
xyz1234567890&$
¢£%ÇØÆŒßço
ăœ̆ fifl ˆ ˇ ˚ (:;,.!?-—""
/#*)[†‡§»«12345
67890]ABCDEFGHIJ
KLMNOPQRSTUV
WXYZ

Book Italic
*ABCDEFGHIJKL
MNOPQRSTU
VWXYZabcdefghij
klmnopqrstuvw
xyz1234567890&$
¢£%ÇØÆŒßço
ăœ̆ fifl ˆ ˇ ˚ (:;,.!?-—""
/#*)[†‡§»«1234
567890]*

Medium
ABCDEFGHIJKL
MNOPQRSTU
VWXYZabcdefgh
ijklmnopqrstu
vwxyz1234567890
&$¢£%ÇØÆŒßß
çoăœ̆œfifl ˆ ˇ ˚ (:;,.!?
-—""/#*)[†‡§»«12
34567890]ABCDEFG
HIJKLMNOPQRST
UVWXYZ

Medium Italic
*ABCDEFGHIJKL
MNOPQRSTU
VWXYZabcdefghij
klmnopqrstuvwx
yz1234567890&$¢
£%ÇØÆŒßçoăœ̆
œ̆fifl ˆ ˇ ˚ (:;,.!?-
—""/#*)[†‡§»«12
34567890]*

Bold
**ABCDEFGHIJKL
MNOPQRSTU
VWXYZabcdefgh
ijklmnopqrstuv
wxyz1234567890&
$¢£%ÇØÆŒßç
oăœ̆œfifl ˆ ˇ ˚ (:;,.!?
-—""/#*)[†‡§»«
1234567890]**

Bold Italic
***ABCDEFGHIJKL
MNOPQRSTU
VWXYZabcdefghij
klmnopqrstuv
wxyz1234567890
&$¢£%ÇØÆ
Œßçoăœ̆œfifl ˆ ˇ ˚ (:;
,.!?-—""/#*)[†
‡§»«]***

Ultra
**ABCDEFGHIJKLMNOPQRSTUVWXYZabcdefghijklmnopqrstuvwxyz1234567890&$¢£%ÇØÆŒçoăœ̆œfifl ˆ ˇ ˚
(:;.!?-—""/#*)[†‡§»«1234567890] "...the beauty and perfection of the Jenson roman is due in part to its imperfection
and inconsistency of details." "...this subtle contrast between similar parts on one letter relative to another is one of the contributing factors to
the mellow appearance of Jenson." ITC Legacy Serif would be classified as an exceptionally sensitive interpretation of an earlier style, while ITC Legacy Sans could only be called an original design statement.**

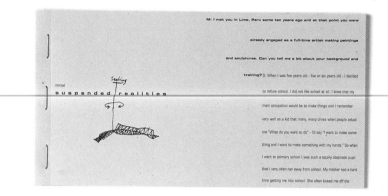

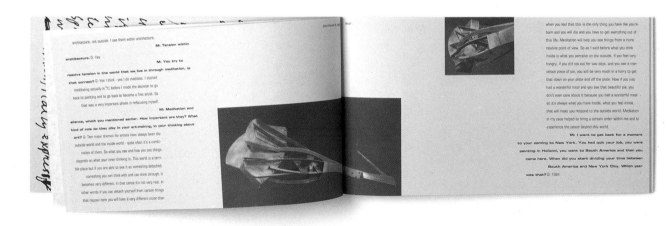

Suspended Realities

Art Director/Studio Nan Goggin/
University of Illinois at Urbana-
Champaign

Designer/Studio Nan Goggin/
University of Illinois at Urbana-
Champaign

Photographers Jos van de
Hamsvoord, Nan Goggin

Illustrator Gam Klutier

Client/Service Krannert Art Museum
and Kinkead Pavilion at the

University of Illinois at Urbana-
Champaign

Paper Simpson EverGreen Text and
Cover, Hickory; Cougar Opaque
White (flyleaf)

Type Eurostile Condensed, Bold and
Extended

Ink Black and silver on off-white

Printing Offset

Software Adobe Photoshop,
QuarkXPress

Concept This catalogue for an exhi-
bition of sculpture by Gam Klutier
echoes the sculptures in its shape and
design: The artist uses large, horizontal pieces of raw wood connected by
silver brackets to create his works,
which are hung from the ceiling
rather than set on the ground. Silver
staples and a flyleaf printed in silver
with a wood pattern allude to the
brackets, while sketches and photographs of Klutier's sculptures are

"suspended" between blocks of type.
The type also escapes its grid at
times, further echoing the shape of
the pieces. Handwriting, enlarged
and reproduced on the inside covers,
adds another human touch.

Cost $2,583

Print Run 1,000

CorVel Corporation 1992 Annual Report

Leading patients through the healthcare system and controlling related costs

Comprehensive managed care services for workers' compensation and group health

Serving the indemnity and employer markets with a national branch network of 82 offices in 40 states

Domino's Pizza implemented CorVel's MedCheck two years ago to manage medical bills, and later added medical case management to enhance its workers' compensation cost containment program.

"We wanted to be absolutely certain that our employees would get the best possible care for their injury.

We had a specific case of assault on one of our drivers and CorVel had an RN case manager there while our employee was still in the emergency room. She was not only able to

"A serious injury affects a lot of people. Not just the worker..." Robert Boik

manage his medical care, but was there to talk to the family." *Robert Boik, Corporate Claims Manager, Domino's Pizza, Inc.*

MedCheck was introduced to Domino's by its third party administrator, ALEXSIS, when the TPA offered CorVel's bill management service to its Fortune 1,000 clientele two years ago. And like Domino's, many employers are adding Advocacy services to lead patients through the entire care episode, from the time of injury.

CorVel Corporation

Design Studio Point Zero
Illustrator Cathy Bleck
Client/Service CorVel Corporation/ managed care
Type Helvetica Extended, Garamond No. 3
Ink Black, teal and match gray on white
Paper Starwhite Vicksburg Text
Printing Offset
Software None

Concept Three scratchboard illustrations are the only artwork in this annual report, which has a clean, uncomplicated look. Text is simple to read, even though some of it is printed in gray on black. The warm, slightly brown-gray is equally readable on black or white. The company's corporate color, teal, is used only for headlines on the financial pages and to list noted company "leaders" on the inside back cover.

Text and Financial Data The first half of the report is all text, distinguished by illustrations, numerous black pages, and a thick, smooth paper stock. The financial data, printed in black on a rough, grayish paper stock, are straightforward. The piece's lack of slick paper and images, and its tall, narrow shape, give it a reassuring, comfortable feel.

Print Run 7,500

John Wong Photography

Art Director/Studio Bryan L. Peterson/Peterson & Co.

Designer/Studio Bryan L. Peterson/ Peterson & Co.

Photographer John Wong

Client/Service John Wong Photography/photography

Paper Mohawk Superfine Cover

Type Handwriting, G9 Gothic No. 3

Ink Black on eggshell

Printing Offset

Software QuarkXPress

Concept This self-promotion piece for an established photographer who left a major photo studio to start his own business relies on the photographer's name and reputation, rather than on explanatory copy, to sell. Props and handwritten "captions" play off Wong's Asian heritage, while a simple announcement on the back cover explains the new business.

Special Production Techniques Black halftones were shot with zero dot in anything lighter than 2 percent or darker than 95 percent black, giving the photographs greater saturation. Uncoated paper, which absorbs ink, adds to the somewhat murky feel.

Cost $1,500

Print Run 1,500

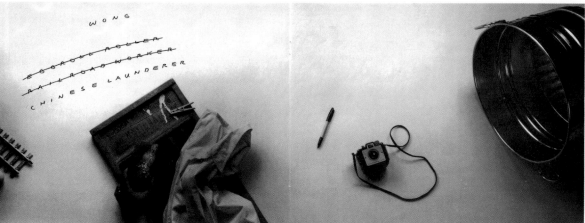

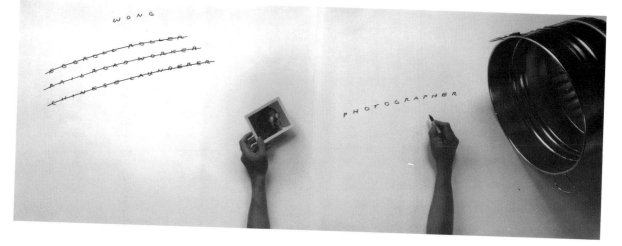

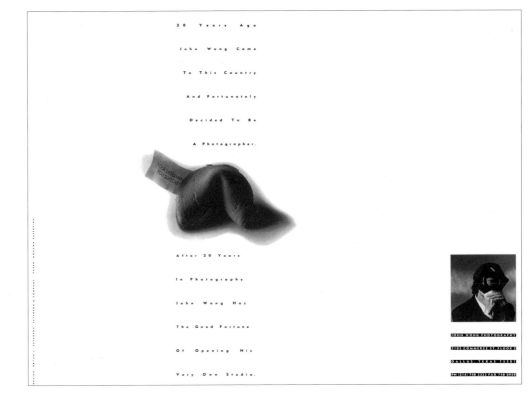

International Typeface Corporation

Art Director/Studio Paul Davis/Paul Davis Studio

Designers/Studio Lisa Mazur, Chalkley Underwood/Paul Davis Studio

Client/Product International Typeface Corporation/type

Paper Newsprint

Type Panache, various

Ink Black on white

Printing Offset

Concept This feature for *U&lc* magazine's twentieth anniversary issue highlights letters designed over the magazine's history, assembling them into a quirky alphabet.

Design Strategy The simple layout highlights the twenty-six very different letters, while giving them nearly equal space. The letter *o* is incorporated into the design of the text, which echoes its shape, while the letter *p* is blown up to fill a page, as if no less space could contain its humorous excess.

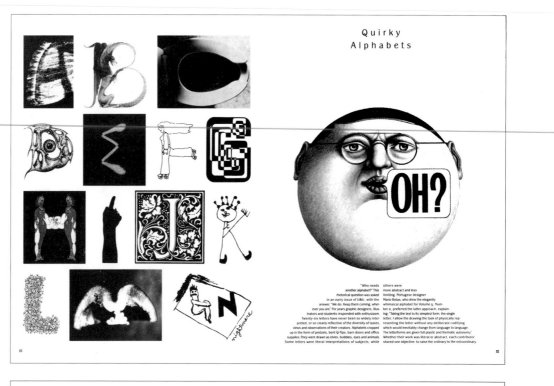

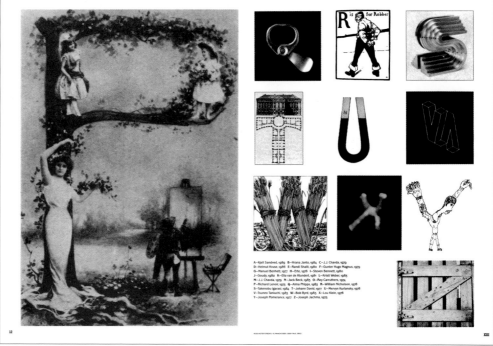

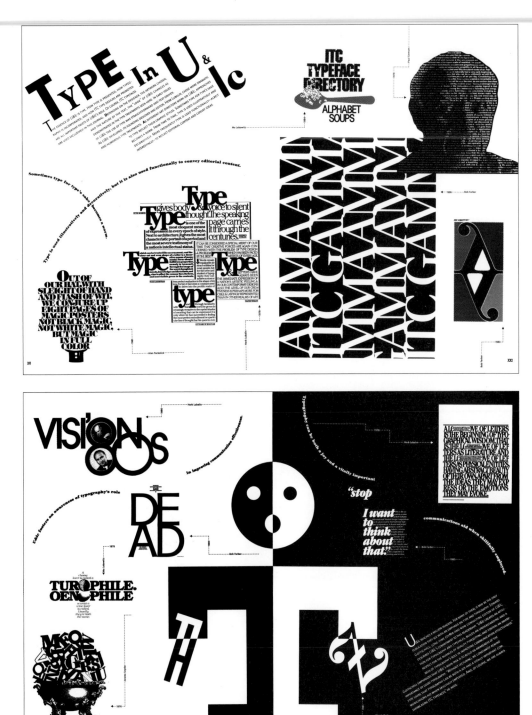

International Typeface Corporation

Art Director/Studio Paul Davis/Paul Davis Studio

Designers/Studio Lisa Mazur, Chalkley Underwood/Paul Davis Studio

Client/Product International Typeface Corporation/type

Paper Newsprint

Type Century, Quay Sans, various

Ink Black on white

Printing Offset

Concept Spreads from a story in the twentieth anniversary issue of *U&lc* magazine show how the publication has presented type since its first issue. The piece highlights the work of past art directors and designers, as well as fashionable type styles of the time. Black and white helps unite these disparate examples, allowing readers to compare and contrast without distraction.

Design Strategy It can be difficult to distinguish copy from illustration when blocks of type are the artwork. The designers used simple sans serif type and dotted lines for credits, and curved lines of bold serif type for captions.

All of the Earth's ecosystems depend on water. Protecting water supplies from pollution and wasteful practices was NRDC's first project, initiated nearly a quarter-century ago. Today we spearhead a coalition of some 400 environmental groups across the country, formed to achieve far-reaching reforms at local, state, and federal levels. ● The Clean Water Act, the cardinal water quality statute of this country, is scheduled for amendment in the coming months. Strengthening it is one of NRDC's highest priorities. Pollution prevention — that is, eliminating hazards before they enter water systems — is a primary goal for our work on the Act as well as in our other scientific, economic, and legal efforts to improve water quality. We are also promoting responsible growth management and efficient land use to reduce polluted stormwater runoff from urban areas. Our campaign to promote conservation of scarce water in the West continues to shape government policies and private business practices. And we remain a driving force in the environmental community's work to restore the integrity of rich coastal systems that support both wildlife and human needs for food, employment, and recreation. For example, NRDC is the main national group working for oil spill prevention and cleanup along the U.S. coast.

Clean Water Act: NRDC has published *The Clean Water Act 20 Years Later*, a comprehensive assessment of the law's successes and failures, which immediately became a keystone of the environmental community's effort to defend and strengthen the law. Authors Bob Adler, Diane Cameron, and Jessica Landman found that the Act has significantly reduced water pollution. Yet they also identified continuing threats: polluted runoff from cities and farms, the primary remaining cause of water quality impairment, hundreds of

millions of pounds of industrial toxic wastes discharged annually; and increasing destruction of wetlands and aquatic ecosystems, with widespread extinction of aquatic species. To solve these problems, NRDC is working for a reauthorized Act that protects damaged watersheds and cuts pollution at the source:

Beach pollution: Coastal pollution threatens the health of beachgoers nationwide, yet the United States does not track the frequency or causes of beach

closings. NRDC fills this gap with *Testing the Waters*, an annual survey to spur public and legislative action to clean up coastal waters. The 1993 edition, by Sarah Chasis and Ashley McLain, found over 2,600 beach closings and contamination advisories during the previous year, most due to raw sewage discharges from outdated sewers, polluted runoff, and inadequate and overloaded sewage treatment plants. To solve these problems, NRDC is seeking stringent pollution prevention measures through the Clean Water Act.

Western water: NRDC scored several successes in a series of lawsuits over flaws in the federal water subsidy program — flaws that have discouraged agricultural water conservation even as drought has overwhelmed the West. These suits complement our efforts to work with irrigators and government in crafting more efficient water policies. The Interior Department settled a suit NRDC had brought to enforce the 960-acre limit on farms receiving cheap federal water. The limit was intended to help small family

farms compete with large agribusinesses, but the Department's regulations have made it virtually meaningless; in the settlement, Interior agreed to rewrite them for all 17 Western states. In another case, the U.S. Supreme Court declined to hear an appeal by California irrigation districts of an earlier NRDC victory, in which the court held that irrigators do not have the right to renew their forty-year water contracts without any environmental review. Finally, a federal court ruled that California's state fishery protection laws apply

to the federal Friant Dam, long a serious impediment to healthy fish populations in the San Joaquin River.

Copalis National Wildlife Refuge: Under pressure from NRDC and a coalition of environmental groups, the U.S. Navy agreed to halt practice bombing runs over a wildlife refuge. Since 1944, the Navy had been dropping inert but smoke-charged bombs from deafening, low-flying A-6 jet war planes into the refuge, a vital coastal breeding ground off

Washington State for seabirds and sea lions. After NRDC filed a lawsuit, the Navy committed to end the bombing runs, and Interior Secretary Bruce Babbitt revoked the letter granting permission.

Wild salmon: Prized Pacific Northwest salmon runs are threatened with extinction by federal hydroelectric and irrigation dams in the Columbia River basin. Karen Garrison and a coalition of environmental groups mobilized public support for adoption of a new regional plan calling for changes in

dam operations to restore salmon. NRDC is now fighting to ensure implementation of that plan, and helping the federal Bureau of Reclamation shape an environmentally responsible program for future water use in the Northwest.

Alaska wetlands: NRDC's Citizen Enforcement Project, created to sue persistent polluters, had more than a dozen successful water pollution cases in 1993. In one of the Project's longest and most important suits, NRDC reached a settlement over the

disposal of massive amounts of toxic waste generated by oil drilling in northern Alaska's tundra wetlands, habitat of many bird species. ARCO Alaska agreed to stop its worst disposal practices, recycle much of the waste, and begin long-term cleanup. ARCO will pay $1 million toward oil cleanup and recycling projects, the U.S. Treasury, and scholarships for Native Alaskans studying environmental protection.

Delaware River: In another major case, NRDC's Citizen

Enforcement Project prevailed over a Texaco refinery regarding its longstanding illegal pollution of the Delaware. NRDC had discovered hundreds of pollution control permit violations at the refinery, some of them exceeding allowable limits by 2,000 percent. The courts responded by levying a fine of over $1.5 million and ordering Texaco to comply with the law. NRDC will carefully monitor Texaco's compliance with the rulings during the coming year.

On The Clean Water Act 20 Years Later: "This fast-moving, clear-eyed book judges twenty tumultuous years of the Clean Water Act and offers an effective law enforcement charter for the future." — RALPH NADER   "An important book at an important time." — VICE PRESIDENT AL GORE

Attorney Hamilton Candee: "His perseverance, combined with unflagging creativity and ingenuity as an attorney, has helped to breathe life into the laws we have long battled to enact." — REP. GEORGE MILLER, CHAIR, HOUSE COMMITTEE ON NATURAL RESOURCES

National Resources Defense Council

Art Director/Studio Jurek Wajdowicz/ Emerson, Wajdowicz Studios, Inc.

Designers/Studio Lisa LaRochelle, Jurek Wajdowicz/Emerson, Wajdowicz Studios, Inc.

Writer Emilie Trautmann

Photographers Richard Elkins (primary), Carl Roodman, Charles Seton

Client/Service National Resources Defense Council/nonprofit environmental organization

Paper Beckett Expressions Snow

Type Adobe Garamond, Franklin Gothic, News Gothic Condensed (customized)

Ink Black and match grays on white

Printing Offset

Software QuarkXPress, Adobe Illustrator

Concept Exciting type treatments, many in white on black, and intriguing nature photography make this annual report for an environmental organization compelling. Unlike annual reports for many private companies, this piece has only two pages of financial data and twelve pages acknowledging donors, board members and staff. Creative use of type is thus paramount in maintaining reader interest. Photos are used sparingly and most kept to less than half a page. However, all are reproduced as tritones for maximum image reproduction quality.

Global

From our earliest days, NRDC has recognized that environmental pollution and ecosystem destruction do not respect national borders. Two decades of international action have strongly positioned us to address today's global environmental challenges. NRDC has been a leader in reforming the environmental policies of U.S. and multilateral foreign aid agencies. In recent years, we have focused on promoting efficiency as an economically and environmentally sound response to the surging energy needs of developing countries, and on promoting "sustainability" as a core objective of U.S. development aid. We expanded this effort in 1993 with the creation of our Population, Consumption, and Environment Initiative to integrate an understanding of sustainability into all our programs. NRDC strives to establish and strengthen critically needed international environmental institutions, to incorporate environmental safeguards into international trade regimes, and to restore U.S. leadership on global environmental issues. We also seek to protect natural resources of international concern, such as the magnificent Bio-Bio River in Chile and the ancient forest of Clayoquot Sound in Canada.

6

Earth Summit aftermath: NRDC helped persuade the new Administration to reverse the United States' defensive posture at the 1992 Earth Summit and take positive actions to follow up on the Summit. For instance, the Administration has now issued a plan for stabilizing carbon dioxide emissions, as specified in the climate change treaty; although the plan calls for voluntary measures, if strongly implemented it could surpass its goal. In addition, Elizabeth Barratt-Brown and Jacob Scherr worked to strengthen the new U.N. Commission on Sustainable Development. At the Commission's first meeting, NRDC released *One Year After Rio*, an unprecedented report on the actions taken by over 80 nations to fulfill the promises made at the Summit. NRDC's Earth Summit Watch project, headed by Scherr and Barrett Frelinghuysen, is pressing the Commission to require mandatory national reporting on environmental progress.

Trade: The negotiations over the North American Free Trade Agreement (NAFTA), begun in 1991, marked a turning point in international trade talks: for the first time, environmental concerns were taken into account, and environmentalists were able to establish an effective voice in the negotiations. Led by John Adams, NRDC played a key role in securing several important advances: pollution cleanup funds for the U.S.-Mexico border; strong provisions to assure that NAFTA will not override or weaken national or state environmental standards; greater rights for citizen participation in environmental policymaking; and a tri-national commission to oversee environmental law enforcement throughout North America. To achieve these successes, Justin Ward, Jacob Scherr, and Lynn Fischer cooperated closely with Mexican and Canadian environmental groups and other U.S. organizations, such as Latino groups.

"NRDC's staff has developed an excellent understanding of environmental issues in Mexico. Their cooperation with the Group of 100 and other Mexican advocates has been important as we work to strengthen environmental protection in Mexico." — HOMER ARIDJIS, PRESIDENT, GROUP OF 100

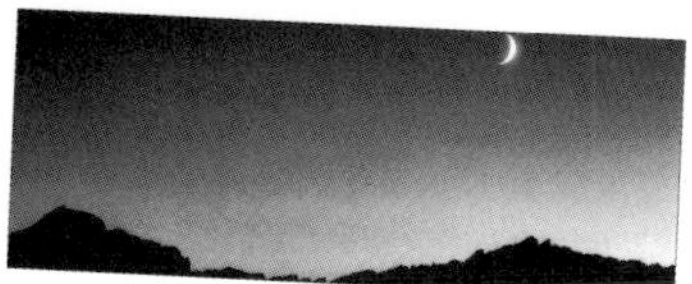

International aid: Sweeping environmental reforms are in store for three development aid institutions with enormous influence on the environment in the developing world, thanks in part to NRDC's advocacy. U.S. AID will place new emphasis on environmentally sustainable development. The World Bank will give peoples affected by its projects greater access to information on those projects and create an independent panel to hear public complaints. And a permanent Global Environmental Facility (GEF) is being restructured to serve as a key funding source for the Earth Summit treaties on climate change and biodiversity. The restructuring stems in part from a study by NRDC and Conservation International showing that the GEF should operate with greater independence from the World Bank and respond more effectively to the concerns of local communities and organizations in developing countries.

Clayoquot Sound: In April, British Columbia opened up 70 percent of the magnificent rainforest of Clayoquot Sound to logging. NRDC immediately targeted the U.S. and Canadian governments and the timber industry in a campaign to protect this ancient forest and the extraordinary range of life it supports. Robert F. Kennedy, Jr., and Elizabeth Barratt-Brown called international attention to the trade conducted in timber from Clayoquot Sound and other ancient forests at the expense of the environment and native land rights. With British Columbia's environmental community and native peoples, NRDC is pressing for stronger forest protection and management standards throughout North America. If we are successful, efforts to save U.S. forests will not be at the expense of other ancient forests beyond our borders.

James Bay: NRDC continues to build on our 1992 success in helping convince New York State to cancel its multibillion-dollar contract to buy power from the proposed second phase of a hydroelectric mega-project in the James Bay wilderness of Quebec. In cooperation with the Cree Indians and Quebec environmentalists, Ashok Gupta is developing innovative alternatives to another proposed power purchase by New York, and Lisa Speer is assisting in a review of the 5,000-page environmental impact statement on the project. Jacob Scherr and Robert F. Kennedy, Jr., are helping Cree leaders to present their case to the U.S. and Canadian public.

Global warming: NRDC was instrumental in promoting development of the climate change agreement at the 1992 Earth Summit, and we led action on the treaty throughout 1993. Elizabeth Barratt-Brown and Daniel Lashof are representing NRDC at negotiations to strengthen the treaty, making the case for stronger commitments by industrialized countries to cut greenhouse gases and for adequate funding for developing countries to participate. NRDC will work on strengthening the treaty throughout 1994 and coming years.

Ozone layer: NRDC continued the key role we have taken during the past several years in securing strong provisions, in both the Clean Air Act and the Montreal Protocol, to phase out chemicals that deplete the Earth's protective ozone layer. In 1991, after the pesticide methyl bromide was discovered to be a potent ozone depleter, Jennifer Curtis and Elizabeth Barratt-Brown began working with other groups to convince EPA to list it formally as an ozone depleter and phase it out. After Turner Odell filed two lawsuits, in 1993 EPA at last issued rules freezing methyl bromide levels until 2001, when all production and use must stop.

Russian environment: One of Russia's first public-interest environmental law organizations, founded with NRDC's assistance in 1990, has filed the country's first lawsuits to enforce pollution controls. Kristen Suokko advised the group, Lawyers for Environment, in bringing the two suits, which address massive sewage and toxic pollution of St. Petersburg waterways. NRDC has also played a leading role in securing and shaping a new federal program to fund joint projects by independent U.S. and Russian organizations to protect the Russian environment.

On One Year After Rio: *"You have performed an invaluable service, particularly to developing countries, by providing a badly needed reference tool. I cannot overstate the importance to us of your continuing this work."* — YOSIWO GEORGE, MICRONESIAN AMBASSADOR TO THE UNITED NATIONS

NRDC is "one of the most effective environmental litigators on the globe." — SAN FRANCISCO CHRONICLE, MARCH 1993
18

Health

Protecting public health is a priority spanning all of NRDC's programs. From our founding to our current campaigns and plans for future action, we seek to uphold the basic right of all people to unpolluted air, water, and food. NRDC pursues our public health goals in partnership with many other environmental and grassroots groups. Prominent among them are children's health advocates and activists who work to redress the disproportionate impact of pollution on communities of color. Our work takes three primary paths: First, we work for efficient new technologies and processes, such as low-chemical-input farming and industrial recycling of toxics, to prevent pollution before it contaminates the environment. Second, we strive to improve the management of toxic substances; for instance, we laid important groundwork in 1993 to strengthen a key federal statute, the Resource Conservation Recovery Act. Third, we work for adequate cleanup of toxic waste sites, not least because the costs of cleanup are a powerful incentive for polluters to develop efficient, low-polluting technologies.

12

Pesticide safety: NRDC's work helped pave the way for the first-ever decision by a U.S. Administration to reduce pesticide use. In *After Silent Spring*, Jennifer Curtis and Tim Profeta detailed the continuing pesticide contamination of the environment, drinking water, and food in the past three decades. In addition, Erik Olson coordinated several environmental, consumer, labor, and public health groups that endorsed an aggressive Pesticide Reform Agenda for the federal government. Less than a week later, the Administration announced a commitment to curtail pesticide use and encourage sustainable agriculture. The announcement came in response to a study by the National Academy of Sciences that confirmed NRDC's long-held position that pesticides in food jeopardize children's health. NRDC is determined to help make the Administration's pledge a reality through environmentally and economically sound reforms.

Superfund: For two years, NRDC has played a leading role in the debate over amending the Superfund law on cleanup of critical toxic sites. We seek to maintain the "polluter pays" principle as an incentive for pollution prevention, to reduce litigation, and to ensure more efficient, quick, and environmentally sound cleanups. We have made headway through the two major national commissions on Superfund, both of which bring together a wide variety of industry, environmental, community, and environmental justice representatives to air their differences and negotiate recommendations. For instance, thanks in part to analyses put forward by John Adams, Linda Greer, Martin McCrory, and Chris Van LobenSels, both commissions have affirmed the principle that the government should be able to require cleanup and recover cleanup costs at a toxic site from any and all of the polluters at that site, regardless of their degree of liability — while offering polluters a quick, straightforward process for dividing the costs among themselves. NRDC also helped secure recommendations for strict cleanup standards and greater participation of affected communities in deciding on cleanup methods, and created a new system for small polluters to resolve their liability early.

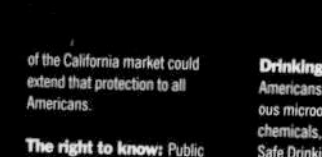

Drinking water: National drinking water protections were strengthened in 1993 because of an NRDC lawsuit. Many states have been ignoring federal drinking water requirements, and, under the previous Administration, EPA declared it had no obligation to demand that states comply with the law. After Erik Olson sued, the court ruled that once EPA finds a state water program to be in violation, it must begin withdrawing federal grants for the program. Already, several states have moved toward full compliance because EPA has put them on notice.

Lead: NRDC won an interim victory in our work to eliminate faucets that leach lead into drinking water—part of our multifaceted collaboration with community and health activists to protect the public, especially children, from lead exposure. Al Meyerhoff, Mitch Bernard, and Erik Olson sued 19 major faucet manufacturers under a California law that sets stringent limits on lead in consumer products. The case has not yet been decided, but the judge has issued a preliminary injunction requiring manufacturers to alert consumers to the risk. If the case leads to a state ban on leaded faucets, the nationwide influence of the California market could extend that protection to all Americans.

The right to know: Public disclosure requirements, which encourage greater environmental responsibility by industry, are a basic right for citizens who may be exposed to pollution. After years of leading the effort to expand the federal "right-to-know" rules to a broader inventory of chemicals and industrial facilities, Deborah Sheiman has won significant progress: EPA has approved our petition to add 11 ozone-depleting chemicals and 23 chronic toxins to the list, and has pledged to add another 313 toxic chemicals. Moreover, in mid-1993, President Clinton extended the right-to-know rules to all federal facilities—and required them to undertake pollution prevention programs, with a recommended reduction of 50 percent.

Drinking water: Millions of Americans are exposed to dangerous microorganisms and toxic chemicals, in clear violation of the Safe Drinking Water Act, because their local water systems do not safeguard water quality. In *Think Before You Drink*, Erik Olson analyzed EPA records of violations by drinking water systems around the country, and outlined the need for a stronger Safe Drinking Water Act, pollution prevention in watersheds, and increased federal funding for water supply monitoring and cleanup (which will create jobs in local communities). The report reached a nationwide audience through front-page newspaper stories and national newscast coverage, and has had a major impact on Congress.

**Groundwater in Hawai`i:** Hawai`i has taken an important step to safeguard its underground water supplies, thanks to NRDC's *Groundwater in Hawai`i*. Authors Laura King and Clyde Murley showed that, while Hawai`i's drinking water remains safe because contaminated wells have been either closed or equipped with treatment plants, Hawai`i lacks a reliable system for detecting contamination and a strong strategy for preventing it. After release of the report and a companion public education brochure, NRDC was able to help arrange an agreement between the state and the U.S. Geological Survey to increase groundwater testing.

Attorney Erik Olson, author of Think Before You Drink: *"He has done a real service for public health in the U.S. His report strikes at the heart of the problem with the water supplies in this country."* — DR. DAVID OZONOFF, CHAIR, DEPT. OF ENVIRONMENTAL HEALTH, BOSTON UNIVERSITY

Earth Technology Corporation

Art Director/Studio Lana Rigsby/ Rigsby Design, Inc.

Designers/Studio Lana Rigsby, Troy S. Ford/Rigsby Design, Inc.

Principal Photographers Gary Faye, Arthur Meyerson

Client/Service The Earth Technology Corporation/environmental, earth sciences and waste management consultants

Paper Centura Dull Cover, Confetti Text (flyleaf)

Type Bodoni, Helvetica Black Extended

Ink Two match blacks, metallic silver, spot dull varnish and four-color process on white

Printing Sheet-fed

Software QuarkXPress

Concept This capabilities brochure for an environmental consulting firm contrasts black-and-white images and text with a central section of color photographs of industrial subjects. The deep black-and-white halftones present the natural world as pristine, while the formal type arrangement adds to the sense of a natural order.

Print Run 5,000

Doing the Right Things. Earth Technology's work is concerned with nothing less than the whole earth: land, air, water, flora, fauna, archeological and cultural artifacts. ▪▪ The projects we undertake today reflect the increasing sweep of the regulatory machine set in motion by the National Environmental Policy Act (NEPA) beginning in the 1970s. ▪▪ Our primary services range from environmental planning and compliance assessment to design and remedial action; site investigations; regulatory program support; waste mini-

BY EVOLVING WITH THE ENVIRONMENTAL INDUSTRY, EARTH TECH- NOLOGY DEVELOPED THE SKILLS, APPROACHES, TECHNOLOGIES, AND SENSITIVITIES MOST LIKELY TO HELP CLIENTS. WE SUPPORT THEM BY CREATING, CLARIFYING, AND MANAGING THE KNOWLEDGE AND RESOURCES THEY NEED TO TAKE THE BEST ACTION FOR THEMSELVES AND THE ENVIRONMENT—SO THEY CAN MAKE DECISIONS CONFIDENTLY.

mization; environmental and safety monitoring; program management; facility closure; asbestos; and environmental data management. ▪▪ We continue to excel in geotechnical services. And we remain a leader in providing site characteri- [z]ation and selection, planning, design, and construction [mana]gement on everything from solid and hazardous waste [contro]ls to advanced defense systems. ▪▪ So while our tech-[nology fo]cus is on the engineering sciences and the technology [areas we] know best, we have adapted our services to fit new [challeng]es faced by our clients in a rapidly changing world.

Coming Clean. Between 1989 and 1991 the EPA recorded total private-party Superfund settlements of $3 billion, exceeding the cumulative total of the prior eight years. This is indicative of a growing pressure on government and industry alike to take environmental action, now. ▪▪ The majority of our work today is in environmental engineering and waste management (solid, hazardous, and medical), from remedial investigations and design to site cleanup, soil and groundwater treatment, operation and monitoring, and health and safety services.

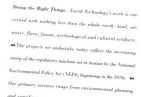

HISTORICALLY, PUBLIC AND PRIVATE SECTORS HAVE FOCUSED ON THE ANALYSIS PHASE OF ENVIRONMENTAL ISSUES. THE DOD AWARDED EARTH TECHNOLOGY A MAJOR BIOREMEDIATION AND SOIL VENTING CONTRACT IN 1992. THIS AND SIMILAR REMEDIAL ACTION CONTRACTS REPRESENTED A NEW DIRECTION: MOVING FULL-BORE INTO CLEANUP. OUR EXPERIENCE WILL BE A KEY IN HELPING ACHIEVE THE MASSIVE EFFORTS AHEAD.

Never have our assignments been more diverse. ▪▪ At one end of the spectrum, we've been responsible for a "simple" tank pull in California (where over 250 different agencies may govern the process) and installing standard pump-and-treat systems. ▪▪ At the other end, we've devised waste minimization programs, remediated contaminated soils, cleaned up fuel spills, designed groundwater remediation systems, and implemented technology such as vapor extraction and bioventing. Decades of working with evolving regulations and technologies have taught us what works and how to move from assessment to action.

International Typeface Corporation

Art Director/Studio Paul Davis/Paul Davis Studio

Designers/Studio Lisa Mazur and Chalkley Underwood/Paul Davis Studio

Client/Product International Typeface Corporation/type

Paper Newsprint

Type Various

Ink Black on white

Printing Offset

Concept Black and white accommodates all the type treatments and illustrations layered in this layout for *U&lc* magazine's twentieth anniversary issue. Letters sent to the magazine over its twenty-year existence were incorporated into two spreads that demonstrate the type of creative correspondence the magazine receives. Color photographs might have made the pieces too difficult to read.

Studio Directory

After Hours Creative
1201 E. Jefferson, 100B
Phoenix, AZ 85034

Charles S. Anderson
Charles S. Anderson
Design Co.
30 N. 1st St.
Minneapolis, MN 55401

Art Direction
10 E. 39th St.
New York, NY 10016

D. Betz Design
2320 1st Ave., Suite 300
Seattle, WA 98121

Bielenberg Design
421 Tehama St.
San Francisco, CA 94103

Stephen Brower Design
31 E. 32nd St., 10th Floor
New York, NY 10016

Pam Cerio Design
7710 Wake Robin Dr.
Cleveland, OH 44130

CFD Design
3333 E. Camelback Rd.,
Suite 200
Phoenix, AZ 85018

**Clarity Coverdale Fury
Advertising, Inc.**
120 South Sixth St.,
Suite 1300
Minneapolis, MN 55402

Concrete®
633 S. Plymouth Ct.,
Suite 208
Chicago, IL 60605

**Concrete Design
Communications Inc.**
2 Silver Ave.
Toronto, ON M6R 3A2
Canada

DL Graphics Studio
6303 E. Halbert Rd.
Bethesda, MD 20817

Paul Davis Studio
14 E. 4th St.
New York, NY 10012

Design!
909 Chattanooga Ave.
Dalton, GA 30720

**Emerson, Wajdowicz
Studios, Inc.**
1123 Broadway
New York, NY 10010

Fallon McElligott
901 Marquette Ave. S.,
Suite 3200
Minneapolis, MN 55402

Philip Fass
1310 State St.
Cedar Falls, IA
50613-4128

Andrea Fridley
238 Powers St.
Brooklyn, NY 11211

GSD&M Advertising
1250 Capital of Texas
Highway S.
Building 1, Suite 400
Austin, TX 78746

Eric Kass Design
9645 Alexander Lane
Fishers, IN 46038

Lord, Dentsu & Partners
810 Seventh Ave.
New York, NY 10019

Lorenc Design
724 Longleaf Dr. NE
Atlanta, GA 30342-4307

Loucks Atalier
20 Greenway Plaza,
Suite 624
Houston, TX 77046

Bernard Maisner
Bernard Maisner Studio
Represented by Gerald &
Cullen Rapp, Inc.
108 E. 35th St.
New York, NY 10016

Joe Miller's Company
3080 Olcott St., Suite 210A
Santa Clara, CA 95054

**Stewart Monderer Design,
Inc.**
10 Thacher St., Suite 112
Boston, MA 02113

**Morrison Design &
Advertising**
2001 Sul Ross
Houston, TX 77098

Pentagram Design, Inc.
620 Davis St.
San Francisco, CA 94111

Peterson & Co.
2200 N. Lamar, 310
Dallas, TX 75202

Point Zero
4223 Glencoe Ave.,
Suite A223
Marina del Rey, CA 90292

Rigsby Design, Inc.
5650 Kirby Dr., #260
Houston, TX 77005

Hal Riney & Partners
735 Battery St.
San Francisco, CA 94111

Rock, Paper, Scissors
619 W. Cornelia St.,
Suite 2
Chicago, IL 60657

Sackett Design Associates
2103 Scott St.
San Francisco, CA
94115-2120

**Mike Salisbury
Communications Inc.**
2200 Amapola Ct., #202
Torrance, CA 90501

Sayles Graphic Design
308 Eighth St.
Des Moines, IA 50309

Toni Schowalter Design
1133 Broadway,
Suite 1610
New York, NY 10010

Segura, Inc.
361 W. Chestnut St.,
1st Floor
Chicago, IL 60610

Shimokochi/Reeves
4465 Wilshire Blvd., #100
Los Angeles, CA 90010

Sommese Design
481 Glenn Rd.
State College, PA 16803

Stowe Design
125 University Ave.,
Suite 220
Palo Alto, CA 94301

Studio MD
1512 Alaskan Way
Seattle, WA 98101

Joel Templin
Templin Design
212 Groveland Ave.
Minneapolis, MN 55403

THARP DID IT
50 University Ave.,
Suite 21
Los Gatos, CA 95030

246 Fifth Design
246 Fifth Ave.
Ottawa, ON K1S 2N3
Canada

**University of Illinois at
Urbana-Champaign**
408 E. Peabody
143 Art and Design
Champaign, IL 61821

Valentine Group
17 Vestry St.
New York, NY 10013

Copyright Notices

Index of Design Firms

Index of Clients

More Great Books for Great Designs!

1996 Artist's & Graphic Designer's Market—This marketing tool for fine artists and graphic designers includes listings of 2,500 buyers across the country and helpful advice on selling and showing your work from top art and design professionals. *#10434/$23.99/720 pages*

Graphic Design: Inspirations and Innovations—Seventy-five of America's top designers discuss how they work, the creative process and the client relationship. Included are discussions on where ideas come from, how to work out your ideas and selling ideas to the client. *#30710/$28.99/144 pages/201 color, 49 b&w illus.*

Graphic Design Basics: Marketing and Promoting Your Work—This practical guide covers the marketing essentials you need to get the word out on your work. Throughout, successful designers share their own "Super Strategies" for marketing—proven ideas on such topics as establishing recognition and avoiding miscommunication with clients. *#30706/$27.99/128 pages/25 color, 10 b&w illus.*

Graphic Design Basics: Creating Logos & Letterheads—Using 14 creativity-sparking, step-by-step demonstrations, Jennifer Place shows you how to make logos, letterheads and business cards that speak out about a client and pack a visual punch. *#30616/$27.99/128 pages/110 color, 125 b&w illus.*

Creating Great Designs on a Limited Budget—This studio manual, written by two authors who know design and its penny-pinching realities, shows designers how to create topflight work, even when the dollars are few. You'll discover how to create impact using only one or two colors, ways to get high mileage from low-cost visuals, thrifty ways to get jobs produced and many other money-saving tips. *#30711/$28.99/128 pages/133 color, 27 b&w illus.*

Graphic Design Basics: Making A Good Layout—Discover how to create more effective layouts that attract the viewer's attention, organize information and fulfill the purpose of the piece. In five highly illustrated chapters, you'll learn how to identify a good layout and how to use the elements and principles of design effectively. Then you'll practice what you learn by working side by side with the authors as they create a sample layout for an actual project. *#30364/$24.99/128 pages/40 color, 100 b&w illus.*

Graphic Edge—This bold international collection explores nontraditional ways of using type. Over 250 color images of typographic rebellions from top designers are presented. *#30733/$34.95/208 pages/280 color illus./paperback*

More Great Design Using 1, 2, & 3 Colors—Make your ideas soar and your costs plummet. Dozens of ingenious examples will help you create great work without four-color expense. *#30664/$39.95/192 pages/225 color illus.*

Quick Solutions to Great Layouts—Get your creative juices flowing with hundreds of time-saving ideas! You'll find sample cases with real-world solutions including full specs for newsletters, brochures, ads and more! *#30529/$24.99/144 pages/200 illus.*

Quick Solutions for Great Type Combinations—When you're looking for that "just right" type combination and you don't have the time or money to experiment endlessly, here are hundreds of ideas to create the mood you're after, including all specs. *#30571/$26.99/144 pages/175 b&w illus./paperback*

Graphic Idea Notebook—This innovative, problem-solving source book for magazine editors and art directors provides over 1,000 editorial design ideas. *#30303/$19.95/206 pages/1,250 b&w illus./paperback*

How to Get Great Type Out of Your Computer—112 time-and-money saving tips for designers and desktop publishers. *#30360/$22.95/138 pages/50 b&w illus./paperback*

Getting Started In Computer Graphics—A hands-on guide for designers and illustrators with more than 200 state-of-the-art examples. Software includes Adobe Photoshop, Fractal Design Painter, Aldus FreeHand, Adobe Illustrator, PixelPaint and Micrografx Designer. *#30469/$27.95/160 pages/125 color, 25 b&w illus./paperback*

Creating Brochures and Booklets—Detailed demonstrations show you precisely how to plan, design and produce everything from a church bulletin to a four-color brochure. Plus, a full-color gallery of 20 well-designed brochures and booklets will give you loads of inspiration. *#30568/$26.99/128 pages/60 color, 145 b&w illus.*

Fresh Ideas in Promotion—Whenever you need a shot of creativity this knockout collection of everything from brochures and newsletters to packaging and wearables will bring you the freshest ideas for a variety of clients (and budgets)! *#30634/$29.99/144 pages/220 color illus.*

Setting the Right Price for Your Design and Illustration—Don't price yourself out of work or vital income. Easy-to-use worksheets show you how to set the right hourly rate plus how to price a variety of assignments! *#30615/$24.99/160 pages/paperback*

Graphic Design Basics: Working with Words & Pictures—Learn how to make type an attractive, effective communication tool and how to use visuals and graphics to beautify and communicate. In 150 examples, you'll discover achievable designs offering instructions and tips you can put to work in your own designs. #30515/$26.99/128 pages/ 32 color, 195 b&w illus.

Getting Unlimited Impact With Limited Color—Discover how to deliver high-impact colors on a budget by mixing two screen tints, replacing 4 color photos with duotones or tritones and dozens of other techniques! #30612/ $27.99/144 pages/120 color illus.

Graphic Artists Guild Handbook of Pricing & Ethical Guidelines, 8th Edition—You'll get practical advice on how to negotiate fees, the ins and outs of trade practices, the latest tax advice and more. #30574/$24.95/240 pages/ paperback

Complete Process Color Finder—Take the guesswork out of color printing jobs. Complete process color samples with graduated tints and shades for each color, enable this guide to provide you with a full range of creative color choices. #30677/$24.99/182 pages/full-color throughout

Using Type Right—121 no-nonsense guidelines for designing with type. Dozens of examples demonstrate good versus bad type design and help you make the statement you want. #30071/$18.95/ 120 pages/paperback

Getting It Printed—Discover practical, hands-on advice for working with printers and graphic arts services to ensure the down and dirty details like consistent quality, on-time output and effective cost control. #30552/$29.99/208 pages/ 134 color, 48 b&w illus./paperback

Make Your Scanner A Great Design & Production Tool—Discover powerful techniques and time-saving tips to help you get quick, clean scans and "just right" images. You'll learn how to make the most of your scanning equipment with step-by-step instructions on everything from cleaning up undesirable moiré patterns to creating special effects. #30661/$27.99/144 pages/117 color, 103 b&w illus./paperback

The Designer's Commonsense Business Book, Revised Edition—Find guidance on setting up shop, networking, pricing, self-promotion and record keeping to help you meet your long-term goals. Completely updated and revised, this book will help you learn the nuts-and-bolts business practices for freelance success. #30663/$27.99/224 pages/paperback

The Graphic Artist's Guide to Marketing and Self-Promotion—Get the most from your efforts and talent! First-hand experiences of other designers and illustrators show you exactly what to do and what to avoid. #30353/$19.99/128 pages/81 b&w illus./paperback

Basic Desktop Design and Layout—This book shows you how to maximize your desktop publishing potential and use any desktop system to produce designs quickly. #30130/$27.95/160 pages/50 color, 100 b&w illus./ paperback

Fresh Ideas in Letterhead & Business Card Design 1—A great idea-sparker for your own letterhead, envelope and business card designs. One hundred twenty sets shown large, in color and with notes on concepts, production and costs. #30660/$29.99/144 pages/325 color illus.

Fresh Ideas in Letterhead & Business Card Design 2—A great idea-sparker for your own letterhead, envelope and business card designs. One hundred twenty sets shown large, in color, and with notes on concepts, production and costs. #30660/$29.99/144 pages/325 color illus.

Collage with Photoshop—Step-by-step demonstrations will show you how to create cutting-edge images using Specular International's image composition software, Collage, with Adobe Photoshop, Fractal Painter and other digital imaging programs. This astonishing collection of projects provides you in-depth instruction and inspiration to absorb into your own digital imaging skills. #30735/ $39.99/205 pages/700 color illus./paperback

Creativity for Graphic Designers—If you're burned-out or just plain stuck for ideas, this book will help you spark your creativity and find the best idea for any project. #30659/$29.99/144 pages/169 color illus.